Word Processing with Amstrad

Other business computer books from Macmillan

Planning for Data Communications
  J. E. Bingham and G. W. P. Davies
The Ultimate Software Selector for Business Micros
  Federation of Micro System Centres
Introduction to Local Area Computer Networks
  K. C. E. Gee
The Computer Handbook: A Businessman's Guide to Choosing and Using Computer Systems
  Charles Jones
Security of Computer Based Information Systems
  V. P. Lane
Understanding Microcomputers
  Dennis Langley
Dictionary of Information Technology
  Dennis Langley and Michael Shain
The Microcomputer Users' Handbook
  Dennis Langley and Michael Shain
Understanding Management Software
  Andrew Leigh
Dictionary of Microcomputing (third edition)
  Charles Sippl

Other books of related interest

Using CP/M
  Peter Gosling
Micro-Maths
  Keith Devlin
Computer Literacy: A beginners' guide
  Vincent Walsh
Sorting Routines for Microcomputers
  Keith McLuckie and Angus Barber
Geometric and Artistic Graphics: Design generation with microcomputers
  Jean-Paul Delahaye
The Future of the Microcomputer in Schools
  Nick Evans
Microchild: Learning through LOGO
  Serafim Gascoigne
The Purple Planet: Micro-PROLOG with the Spectrum 48K
  Serafim Gascoigne
Turtle Fun: LOGO for the Spectrum 48K
  Serafim Gascoigne
Advanced Graphics with the IBM Personal Computer
  Ian O. Angell
Programming in Z80 Assembly Language
  Roger Hutty
Mastering Computers
  G. G. L. Wright
Mastering Computer Programming
  P. E. Gosling
Mastering Data Processing
  J. Bingham
Mastering COBOL
  R. Hutty
Mastering Pascal Programming
  E. Huggins

Word Processing with Amstrad
The PCW8256/8512

Ron Hughes

MACMILLAN

First published 1986

Published by
MACMILLAN EDUCATION LTD
Houndmills, Basingstoke, Hampshire RG21 2XS
and London
Companies and representatives
throughout the world

Printed in Great Britain by
Camelot Press Ltd,
Southampton

British Library Cataloguing in Publication Data
Hughes, Ron
   Word processing with Amstrad:
   The PCW 8256/8512.
   1. Amstrad PCW8256 (Computer)   2. Word
   processing
   I. Title
   652'.5'02854165   Z52.5.A4
   ISBN 0–333–42792–0

Contents

Preface

Whether you are using an Amstrad PCW8256 or PCW8512 now, or plan to sometime in the future, you will find something of interest in this book. As the PCW is a microcomputer that is intended to be used mainly as a word processor, this book is primarily a guide to using the word processing software called **LocoScript**, which is supplied with it. While this book mainly concentrates on LocoScript, it also contains essential information on the use of the disk drive(s) and the printer.

A word processor (or WP) is a system which enables you to prepare professional-looking documents via a keyboard and visual display unit (or VDU). You create your document and make any corrections or alterations on the screen and only print it when it is ready. The main advantage is that a copy of your document can be saved on disk and recovered later. Once a document has been saved on disk it can be used over and over again in its present form or be modified to suit the occasion. For example, if you regularly need to send letters to chase customers for payment, you could create a standard letter and then need only add the customer's name and address (not forgetting the date), before printing it.

WPs have been used in industry for some years now, but they have always been very expensive (often costing thousands of pounds). Now, with powerful low cost machines like the PCWs, people from all walks of life can reap the benefits of using a WP, including people who run small businesses, lecturers, authors, etc. This book was written entirely using a PCW8256 with a single disk drive and LocoScript; indeed it is hard to imagine writing a book these days without using a WP!

In an age when it is easy to be dazzled by the vast range of computers competing in the market place, it is comforting to know that these are popular machines, destined to become a major landmark in computing history together with the Sinclair Spectrum and the IBM Personal Computer. Any machine which sells in very large numbers is bound to be well supported with software. Here for the first time is a WP that includes a monitor, disk drive and printer at a cost which is less than some WP packages alone! But the PCW is in fact much more than a dedicated WP, it includes the CP/M Plus operating system which enables it to perform many different tasks by running other applications programs such as spreadsheets, database systems, etc.

This book assumes no prior level of knowledge or computer literacy. If you are still at the stage where you think that bytes are what you get from fleas and that RAM is a male sheep, then you will be relieved to learn that all jargon and technical terms like this will be fully explained!

However, it is asssumed, if you are using a PCW, that you have Locomotive Software's LocoScript v 1.2, CP/M Plus v 1.4 and the first edition (1985) of the Amstrad Book 1 *'User Guide - CP/M Logo & Word Processor Manual'*. If you have an earlier version of LocoScript or CP/M Plus then you should return the master disk to Amstrad who should replace it with the current version, free of charge.

While you might want to read this book from cover to cover you may find it useful to browse through it before doing so, to get used to its layout and to be able to find your way around in it. In a book of this type you will need to be able to find pieces of information after you have read it, so it has been organised with this thought in mind; you should find the cross references it contains useful.

Every effort has been made to ensure accuracy in this book, as it is fully appreciated that errors can very easily destroy a beginner's fragile confidence. However, if you have a later version of this software or a later edition of Amstrad's Book 1, then you might find some inconsistencies with this book. Nevertheless, the greater part of this book should remain relevant to future versions.

The following conventions are used in this book:

> angled brackets signify a single key to be pressed, e.g. <RETURN> or <Y>

> <[≡]> represents the key located between <←> and <→>

> <[+]> and <[-]> are used to represent the *Set* and *Clear* keys at either end of the space bar

> ⊗ represents the tick that is sometimes displayed against an option in some of the pull-down menus and used to indicate your choice

> text enclosed between ⇒ and ⇐ represents the option in a pull-down menu which will be selected if you press <ENTER>

Acknowledgements

I owe thanks to the late Edwin Clarke who first kindled my interest in the PCW8256, Vic Pearson who persuaded me to take the plunge and spend my hard-earned cash on one, and Bob Hill, Martin Roberts and Bob Hersee for their encouragement. My thanks also go to my wife Liz, without whose support, proofreading and endless cups of coffee this book would never have reached fruition, and also to our children Laura and Melvyn for endeavouring to keep the ambient noise level below 120dB! Also, thanks to Malcolm Stewart and Jon Finegold of Macmillan Education Ltd for their help and ideas during the publishing of this book. Finally, the greatest credit must go to Amstrad for producing such excellent machines.

Ron Hughes
Findon
Summer, 1986

1 Introducing the Word Processor

1.1- WHY USE A WORD PROCESSOR?

Word processors are used because they not only provide more elegant solutions to the age-old problems of error correction and making extra copies but they can be made to perform lots of other clever tricks as well. For example, some word processors allow you to merge a list of names and addresses with a standard letter so that you can manufacture personalised letters very quickly.

Word processors usually allow you to control the layout (or format) of your documents. For example, an article that you might want to prepare for a magazine column, would obviously have to be printed in a narrower format than say, a letter.

In addition to this many word processors enable you to change the style of your text. For example, you might want to have certain words in your document printed in italics, or you might want to have all your headings in a report appear in bold print. Word processors enable you to do this by placing special commands in your text which instruct the printer to change to italic or bold print, etc. These commands are called *embedded control codes*.

Another thing that you can normally do with a word processor is move a block of text (e.g. a paragraph) to a different location in a document. Alternatively, you could delete the block if you wanted to. When you carry out this kind of task the word processor will automatically close up the gap that is left when you move or delete the block. It will also make room for the block when you reinsert it elsewhere, keeping the layout of the rest of the document intact.

Word processors will perform lots of other tasks for you quite tirelessly. For example, if you were writing a book about Turkey, you might make reference to Byzantium, and elsewhere in the book cover the development of modern Istanbul. Later, if you wanted to replace earlier occurrences of the word Istanbul with Constantinople, you could do that quite easily by means of a special search and replace facility.

Some word processors even provide a dictionary so that you can get the computer to check your text for spelling mistakes. Spelling-checkers, often have a dictionary of 20,000 words or more. Most spelling-checkers enable you to add to the dictionary, so you can add words for use in your own specialised field of interest. It is even possible to get a computer to generate an index for a book, automatically.

It's not unusual for word processors to provide a word-count facility so that you can keep track of the size of your document.

1.2 - ARE ALL WORD PROCESSORS THE SAME?

There are two different types of word processor:

> (1) there are *dedicated word processors* (e.g. like the PCW) which are specifically designed for the job. Dedicated word processors generally have a display screen, keyboard, disk storage system and printer. Together these parts are referred to as the *hardware*. The keyboard usually has some special keys which are used just for word processing. The PCW is unusual, in that unlike other dedicated word processors, it can also be used for other jobs. Its word processing software, **LocoScript**, is supplied on a disk.

> (2) word processing programs are readily available for most programmable computers; given a disk drive (or cassette recorder), printer and this software, they can then be used as a word processor. Programs are sometimes called *software*. The word processing software might be made available on cassette tape, disk or in a special memory chip. Some home computers have numbered function keys and these are then programmed to act like dedicated word processing keys.

The various dedicated word processing systems that are available fall into three main categories:

> (1) stand-alone systems which support one operator. The PCW is a stand-alone system.

(2) networked systems which enable several operators to share printers and files. Given the appropriate interfaces and programs it is possible to connect the PCW to other microcomputers like the BBC Model B, Apple II/IIe, IBM PC and Apricot. This is a bit like a daisy chain, and is called a network. In a networked system a number of microcomputers can be connected together so that data can be passed between them. The advantage is that expensive resources like disk drives and printers can be shared between them. They are then called *shared resource systems*.

(3) hybrid systems attached to a central mainframe or minicomputer, which are able to perform additional functions such as accessing large databases. It is possible to connect the PCW to computer systems such as Prestel. To be able to do this you will need a suitable interface, special software and a device called a modem. A modem (*modulator/demodulator*) converts the signal from a computer into a form which can be transmitted along a telephone line. If the computer at the other end of the line is also connected to a modem, and has the right interface plus software, then they will be able to communicate with each other. It will then be possible to exchange documents or other data. You are not just limited to communicating with other computers in this country; if you can afford the telephone charges then you can link up to computers in other parts of the world!

Word processors usually provide the following features:

document creation and editing, including the ability to:

(a) insert, delete, copy, and move text around in a document.

(b) include text and/or graphics from other documents.

(c) search for and replace strings of characters in the document.

document formatting and printing using a choice of paper sizes and formats with multiple copies as required.

text justification to specified margins with automatic hyphenation.

ability to create a document from a standard template, e.g. one containing a company letter heading.

use of alternative character sets such as bold, italic, underlined, etc.

layout of tables, figures, etc.

substitution of variable information when printing the document for easy production of form letters, etc.

In order for a computer to be able to use a disk drive it must have a special program called a Disk Operating System (DOS) which is usually supplied on a disk. The PCW is supplied with an industry standard DOS, called CP/M. The fact that CP/M is an industry standard means that there are literally thousands of software packages already in existence which will run under CP/M. The PCW should be able to use many of these software packages, although some of them may need to be specially adapted. They will also have to be converted to the machine's 3-inch disk format as most of them are configured for the industry standard 5¼-inch disk. Increasingly, many of these software packages are being made available to run on the PCW, for less than the cost of equivalent packages for other computers.

When the machine is being used as a dedicated word processor, LocoScript provides its own DOS and therefore CP/M is not used.

Word processors use different kinds of printers:

dot matrix printers use a printhead which contains needles that are 'fired' against the ink ribbon, in order to form the outline of the letters which are made up from a series of dots. *Near letter* quality (NLQ) print is often produced by making a second pass for every line that is printed. Single pass printing tends to be called *draft* quality. The speed varies from about 15 characters per second (cps) to about 350 cps, depending on the cost of the printer and whether you use the draft or NLQ modes. The PCW's printer provides NLQ at about 20 cps or draft quality (single-pass) at about 90 cps. This is slower than average. Dot matrix printers tend to be noisy. It is possible to fit a different printer to the PCW but this requires an optional printer interface (this is described in Chapter 5.1.2).

daisy wheel printers use a printhead which 'fires' a hammer against a daisy printwheel. Each 'petal' of the printwheel has a character on it so that when it is struck by the hammer it is pressed against the ink ribbon and hence forms the image of the character on the paper. These printers produce high quality print but are expensive and tend to be very noisy. Daisy wheel printers, with a speed of about 20 to 55 cps, are slower than most dot matrix printers.

thermal printers, which burn the shapes of the characters on to specially coated paper, are not suitable for serious word processing despite being cheap and quiet, as they produce poor quality print and use more expensive paper.

ink jet printers and laser printers are fast and quiet, but very expensive.

Sometimes noisy printers are housed under special acoustic hoods to keep the noise level within acceptable limits.

Some printers will only handle continuous tractorfed stationery. This is paper which has sprocket holes down the sides and is perforated so that it can be separated into single sheets. It is possible to get this paper with micro-dot perforations down the side, so that when the perforated edges have been removed it is barely distinguishable from a normal sheet of paper. Other printers will accept either single sheets or continuous stationery. Printers which handle single sheets have a platen like that of a typewriter and are called friction feed printers. The PCW's printer will handle both single sheets and continuous stationery.

1.3 - WHAT NEXT?

The purpose of this chapter has been to introduce you to word processing.

Before you start using the PCW in earnest, you should learn how to use and take care of disks. The fruits of your labours with the word processor will be stored on disks and therefore time spent getting to grips with this subject now will save time and heartache later. Chapter 2 is devoted entirely to the use of disks.

Chapter 3 will help you to get to know the PCW and LocoScript. It covers the majority of things that you can do with LocoScript and should give you a good idea of just how easy it is to use a word processor. This book contains lots of examples and explains many of the error messages that you are likely to come across. It should help clarify many of the points that you find difficult. However, just reading the book alone is not enough, you will need to practise using LocoScript.

Chapter 4 is all about the printer. You will probably find that you need to refer to this chapter now and again as you work your way through Chapter 3.

Chapter 5 explains some of the more technical aspects of the PCW and should help to fill in any gaps in your knowledge.

You might find the names and addresses and list of software in the appendices useful and there is a glossary to help you with terms or jargon that you don't understand.

It is assumed that you have read Chapter 1 in Amstrad's Book 1, entitled *'Setting up'*, which is supplied with the PCW, and that you have connected up the machine as described. It is very important that you do NOT use the master disks that are supplied with the PCW for your day-to-day work; you should always use a working copy of LocoScript. If you haven't already made working copies of your master disks, then please read Chapter 2 of this book, which tells you how to do this.

SUMMARY

- A Word Processor (i.e. WP) is a computer which is designed for writing, storing, editing, retrieving and printing documents.
- WP's usually comprise a display screen, QWERTY keyboard, disk drive(s) and printer; this is called the hardware.
- When you use a WP, what you type appears on the screen; you have to instruct it to print your document.
- When your document has been stored on disk it can be retrieved and edited or printed as often as you like.
- WP's make the job of controlling layout and style easy.

- The special codes that you insert in your document to control the printer (but which themselves are not printed) are called embedded control codes.
- WP's enable you to insert, move and delete text within your document quite easily.
- Most WP's provide a search and replace facility to enable you to swap every occurrence of one word with another.
- Most computers can be also be used as a WP; some computers are dedicated word processors.
- The programs which make the computer work are collectively called the software.
- WP's are either stand-alone, networked or hybrid systems.
- Some WP's use templates to produce documents that have a standard layout.
- The PCW uses an industry standard DOS which is called CP/M Plus; it is supplied on a 3-inch disk.
- The WP software is called LocoScript.
- WP's use dot matrix, daisy wheel, ink jet or laser printers. Printers can usually handle continuous and/or single sheet stationery.

2   Using Compact Floppy Disks

One of the main advantages of a word processor over a
typewriter is that some time after producing your documents, if
you need to edit or print them again, there is no need type
them in again, you can simply retrieve the original copy and
make any changes that might be required, like changing the
date. You can also print as many copies as you want, whenever
they are needed, without having to use carbon paper or a
photocopier.

The PCW stores the part of the document that you are
working on in its memory, and this will be safe provided that
you don't change to doing something else, reset the computer,
or switch it off. The computer's memory is volatile and
therefore you should think of it as being only a temporary
storage place.

In order to store a document more permanently you must
get the computer to save it on a disk by using a disk drive.
The method for storing and retrieving documents this way will
be described later, but first you need to learn something about
the disks themselves.

The very first disks to be used were large thin flexible
8-inch disks in cardboard sleeves, hence the name floppy. The
8-inch floppy disk has now been largely superseded by the
5¼-inch floppy disk, which is similar and is still widely used.

Most modern microcomputers like the PCW use a smaller
disk which is enclosed in a rigid plastic housing and
incorporates a shutter mechanism to protect the surface of the
disk itself. Amstrad has settled on the 3-inch disk for use
with its computers. Because 3½-inch disks are popular with a
number of other computer manufacturers, some people believe
that the 3-inch disk is non-standard. A new industry standard
hasn't yet emerged. At the time that this book was being
written, the Financial Times newspaper reported that 50,000

8

PCW's were being produced per month for the world market,
which means that a lot of people will be using 3-inch disks!

These so-called 3-inch disks are enclosed in housings
which are about 3.15" (80mm) wide and 3.94" (100mm) long and
0.2" (5mm) thick, and are called Compact Floppy Disks. The disk
itself is circular and is enclosed for protection. See Figure 1.

Some disks have their sides labelled 1 and 2 whereas
others are labelled A and B.

Both sides of the disks can be used to store programs or
data, but as Drive A (i.e. the upper disk drive) is only capable
of reading one side of a disk at a time, the disk has to be
flipped over before this drive can read the other side; each
side is independent of the other. However, Drive B (i.e. the
lower disk drive) is capable of reading both sides of the
special disks that it uses.

2.1 - TAKING CARE OF DISKS

2.1.1 - Blank disks

You will need to purchase some new blank disks in order to be
able to make working copies of your master disks. Make sure
you specify that they are for use with the PCW. Your computer
dealer should be able to supply you with disks. You will need
at least two blank disks, three would be better; they are quite
a lot cheaper when bought in quantities of ten or more. Drive A
uses CF2 (or CF-2) disks, whereas Drive B uses CF2-DD
(i.e. Double Density) disks. When buying disks make sure that
you get a branded make (e.g. Amsoft, Panasonic, Maxell, Tatung,
etc.); be wary of buying unbranded disks as they might be
unreliable.

Disks are supplied in transparent plastic cases, which in
turn are sealed in cellophane wrappers. Obviously the
cellophane wrappers can be discarded, but you should retain the
plastic cases. Keeping disks in their cases protects them from
dirt and dust when they are not being used. A disk must be
removed from its case before it can be inserted into the disk
drive.

Some people have difficulty opening these cases; the fact
that there are two different types, just adds to the confusion.

Disks which are labelled **A** and **B** are supplied in cases which are slightly wider and shorter. These cases open at the end.

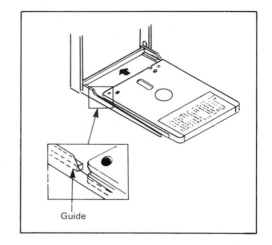

Guide

Disks which are labelled **1** and **2** are supplied in cases which are slightly narrower and longer. These cases open at the side.

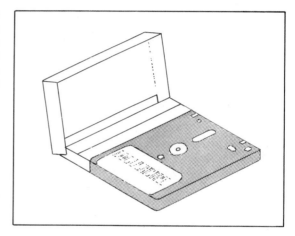

To avoid confusion you might like to place a small self-adhesive label on the case, closest to the end where it opens. A useful extension to this idea would be to use coloured labels to colour code your disk cases. Do NOT place additional labels on the disks themselves, in order to avoid damaging the disk drive.

2.1.2 - Disk construction

The disk itself is a very thin piece of circular polyester, which is a plastic material, and is coated with an extremely thin layer of a magnetic material (similar to the coating on magnetic tape in a music cassette). Both the disk itself and its coatings can be very easily damaged, which is why it is enclosed in a rigid plastic housing.

Because data or programs are recorded on the disk surface magnetically, they be can be easily corrupted by an uncontrolled magnetic field.

If allowed to, dust and dirt can also damage your disks. More seriously it can damage the read/write head in the disk drive. A minute scratch on the surface of the disk is all that is needed to make it incapable of being read properly. While it can be costly and extremely inconvenient if a lot of data is lost in this way, it can be even more expensive if the read/write head in the disk drive is damaged.

Remember that plastic materials often become charged with static electricity which causes them to attract dust; you should avoid subjecting your disks to dusty environments for this reason.

Avoid touching the metal shutter and NEVER touch the surface of a disk itself. The oils which make up a finger-print form a sticky surface which attracts dust. When you insert the disk in the drive you will transfer the dust into the drive.

Extremes of temperature and humidity can also damage your disks by damaging the delicate magnetic coating.

2.1.3 - How to avoid problems

In order to avoid trouble the best course of action is to follow a few basic rules:

- Do NOT open the shutter and touch the magnetic surface of the disk.

- Do NOT press on the shutter or put any heavy object on the disk.

- Do NOT deform the hub.

•   Do NOT place the disk near dust or dirt. Smoke particles can damage your disks.

•   Do NOT attempt to insert anything into the disk.

•   Do NOT insert anything into the disk drive except disks. Keep small children away from the disk drive as they love to 'post' little things into awkward places!

•   Do NOT store disks where they will get damp, get very hot or get very cold. That includes leaving them in a car, on window sills, near radiators or in direct sunlight.

•   Do NOT place disks anywhere near a magnet or strong magnetic field. Most motors and loudspeakers and some telephones contain permanent or electro-magnets. Magnetic fields can also be found at the back of monitors and TV's. Many metal tools like screwdrivers become self-magnetised. Beware of desk top gadgets for keeping paper clips tidy!

•   Do NOT switch the computer on or off when a disk is present in the disk drive.

•   Do NOT attempt to remove a disk while the drive motor is still running. You might be able to hear the drive when it is reading from or writing to the disk; the red indicator lamp on the drive lights brightly or flashes on and off when the drive is reading or writing. Also, if you look at the top right-hand corner of the screen you will see *Using A* (or *Using B*) displayed when Drive A (or Drive B) is being used. Do NOT attempt to remove the disk when either of these messages is being displayed.

You should always treat disks as your most precious possessions. While disks are somewhat delicate, provided you treat them properly they are a convenient and reliable method of storing data.

2.1.4 - Write protecting disks

Your master software disks have been modified physically in such a way as to prevent the computer's disk drive from destroying the programs stored on them. The disks are said to be *write protected*. In computing the process of recording data (information) or programs on the surface of a disk is called writing (or saving).

This is very similar to the write protection system which is used with audio or video cassettes. When the write protect tabs are present, the cassette/video player is free to record on the tape; by breaking them you can prevent what is already recorded on the tape from being destroyed.

Unlike cassettes, the write protection system provided on 3-inch disks is easily reversible. The disks have write protect holes, which are positioned in two corners of the the disk. If you hold a disk by its label then you will see that the two corners which are the furthest from your hand each contain two holes. The smallest of the two, in each corner, is the write protect hole. The left-hand write protect hole is used to protect the side of the disk that you are looking at. The other write protect hole provides protection for the other side of the disk.

When a write protect hole is open, that side of the disk is write protected (the other side might not be). Any attempt to write to that side of the disk will result in a message like this:

Disc write protected

When a write protect hole is closed, that side of the disk can be written to and the disk is said to be *write enabled*.

Disks which are labelled 1 and 2 have tabs on their sides, which can be used to open and close the write protect holes by sliding them back and forth with your thumbnail (these disks also have **A** and **B** moulded near the write protect tabs). Some disks with software on them are supplied with these tabs permanently removed.

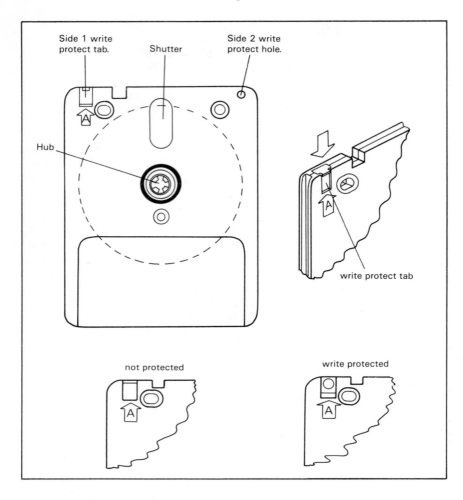

Disks which are labelled **A** and **B**, have small levers set
into the edges of the disk which can be moved laterally with,
for example, the aid of the tip of a ball-point pen.

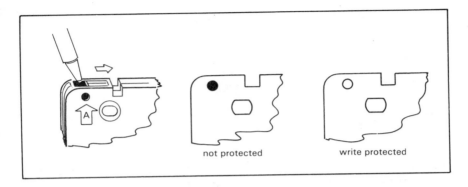

not protected   write protected

WARNING - In order to avoid the accidental loss of the programs from your master disks, or any other software that you buy, you should make sure that the write protect holes are ALWAYS kept open.

When using a LocoScript disk which has been write protected, if you attempt to edit a document then the following message will be displayed on the screen:

```
ERROR in: Edit document
Disc is write protected
→ ● Send result to Drive M:        ←
Cancel operation
Disc write enabled: continue
```

Note that this occurs when you first attempt to edit the document; LocoScript forces you to acknowledge that the disk is write protected and asks you to confirm that you want any edited versions to be saved to Drive M instead of a physical drive. Drive M is a section of the computer's memory that can be used somewhat like another disk drive.

If you choose to *Send the result to Drive M* by pressing <ENTER> then the edited version will be stored in Drive M but lost when the PCW is switched off or reset. The <ENTER> key is located in the bottom right-hand corner of the keyboard.

If you want to abandon editing altogether press <↓> once, to move the menu cursor down to *Cancel operation* and then press <ENTER>; pressing <CAN> has the same effect. Do NOT *write enable* your *master disk*. The <↓> key is located immediately to the left of <ENTER>. The <CAN> key is located in top row of the keyboard; the fourth key in from the right-hand end.

Note that this error message is in fact a menu with a number of options in it.

You will find that LocoScript makes extensive use of menus like this. Some of these menus can be invoked by the single press of a key and appear to scroll down the screen a bit like a roller blind, hence they are called pull-down menus. For example, pressing <f5> invokes the *Rename* menu. Pull-down menus like this can normally be CANcelled by pressing <CAN>. The <f5> key is located in the same column as <CAN>.

Generally speaking these pull-down menus are displayed, highlighted in reverse video, with one line which represents the current option displayed normally (i.e. not in reverse video). This line is called the *menu* cursor and is depicted in this book by means of the symbols ⇥ and ⇤. In some of these pull-down menus you will find that the *menu* cursor can be moved down and back up by means of the appropriate cursor control keys (i.e. <↓> and <↑>). These keys are located in the bottom right-hand corner of the keyboard.

Sometimes a tick will be displayed in the *menu* cursor; at other times a tick will be displayed elsewhere in the menu. In some menus you will find that this tick can be toggled on and off by means of the *Set* and *Clear* keys. These special keys are located at either end of the space bar (i.e. <[+]> and <[-]> respectively). Whenever there is a tick in a menu or in a *menu* cursor you will find it depicted in this book by the ⊕ symbol.

If this all sounds a bit confusing, don't worry. Whenever a *menu* cursor can be moved up and down, this will be made clear; if the tick can be turned on or off this will also be mentioned. You will find that there are lots of example menus in this book and any quirks are explained.

For now just remember:

⇥ represents a *menu* cursor ⇤
⊕ represents a tick

2.2 - THE MASTER SOFTWARE DISKS

Two disks are supplied with the PCW:

Disk 1 Side 1 LOCO SCRIPT v 1.2
Side 2 CP/M PLUS v 1.4

Disk 2 Side 3 PROGRAMMING UTILITIES
Side 4 DR.LOGO & HELP

These *master disks* contain the programs which will make the PCW work. The machine will not work without them, so take good care of them! These are 3-inch Compact Floppy disks or CF2 disks.

If you find that you have a different version of LocoScript from that shown above, don't worry. It is not unusual for software like LocoScript to be re-released with improvements or corrections soon after its initial release.

If side 1 is not version 1.2 (or if side two is not version 1.4) then you should return this master disk to Amstrad, who should replace it with the current version, free of charge.   LocoScript version 1.0 contains a number of bugs (mistakes) in the software, which prevents it from working properly. Take care to make a working copy of LocoScript before you return the master disk to Amstrad, so that you have something to work with in the meantime; Chapter 2.5.3 explains how to do this.

You can check which version you have by following the instructions in Chapter 2.4. Note that some LocoScript master disks have the version number printed on the label. More recently others have been supplied once again without this information, nevertheless they are version 1.2. These disks have a red label stuck onto the transparent disk case.

If you are still using LocoScript version 1.0 you will find that when using the standard template called MANUSCRP, which Amstrad provide, you are prevented from creating a document which is more than 6 pages in length. This version also prevents you from printing individual pages of a document. These and other bugs have been eradicated from the software, hence version 1.0 is obsolete and has been replaced by version 1.2. Two other versions have been seen (i.e. 1.04 and 1.1) but at the time of writing this book version 1.2 was current.

Version 1.2 allows you to:

> (1) print selected pages from within a document (see Chapter 4.2.5 and 4.3)

> (2) prepare an ASCII file from any LocoScript document (see Chapter 2.7.1.7)

You will need to make working copies of these *master disks* and then put them away somewhere safe. Make sure you use the working copies on a day-to-day basis, and NOT the master disks.

2.3 - INSERTING AND REMOVING DISKS

If there is already a disk in the drive, make sure that you
remove it before switching on the PCW. This can be achieved by
pressing the *disk-eject* button which is located in the top
right-hand corner of the disk drive. When you have done that,
press the *Power* button, which is located below the bottom
left-hand corner of the screen. This will switch on the
machine, assuming of course that it is plugged into the mains.
The screen should then light up all over, in a bright green
colour.

To insert a disk in the drive:

> When you remove the disk from its transparent case
> make sure that you hold it by its labelled end so
> that you don't accidentally touch the shutter
> mechanism.
>
> Holding the disk, with the side that you want to use
> to the left (i.e. closest to the screen), insert it
> into the disk drive by pushing it gently into the
> slot until it clicks home. If you feel any
> resistance, don't force it. Try again, after pressing
> the eject button. If you have any difficulty seek
> help from your local computer dealer.

To remove a disk from the drive:

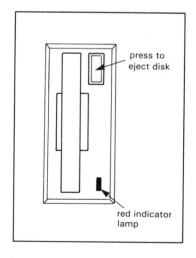

press to
eject disk

red indicator
lamp

> Check that the disk
> drive indicator lamp
> is not brightly lit
> and that *Using A* or
> *Using B* is not
> displayed in the
> *Control zone*.
>
> Press the eject
> button gently but
> firmly (if you press
> it too vigorously
> your disk might pop
> out faster than you
> expect!) and then
> pull the disk out
> gently.

WARNING - Always check to see if there is a disk
in the drive before you switch the PCW on or off; if there is
then make sure you remove it before using the power switch.

2.4 - LOADING LOCOSCRIPT INTO THE PCW's MEMORY

Insert the disk, with the side containing LocoScript nearest to the screen, into the upper drive. The screen will clear momentarily and you might be able to hear the drive motor gently whirring. You will see the disk drive's light flashing on and off as the disk is read, and then a pattern of black horizontal lines will begin to fill the screen, followed briefly by:

AMSTRAD PCW8256 Personal Computer Word Processor
Locomotive Software's LocoScript v 1.20
© 1985 Locomotive Software Ltd. & Amstrad Consumer Electronics plc

If you don't insert a disk, then within about one and a half minutes of switching on the PCW, it will beep at you impatiently. If it does beep before you get a chance to insert your disk, then you will need to press the space bar, after inserting the disk, to get it to load LocoScript; otherwise it will be more friendly and load LocoScript automatically without any further prompting from you. You will see the print head, on the printer, move briefly to the right and then back to the left again.

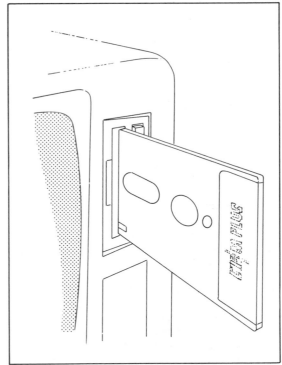

Insert your master disk which contains LOCOSCRIPT and CP/M PLUS into Drive A with CP/M (i.e. side 2) facing left (towards the screen).

If you have inserted the wrong side of the disk, you will see a message like this displayed:

```
CP/M Plus Amstrad Consumers Electronics plc
v 1.4, 61K TPA, 1 disc drive, 112K drive M:
A>_
```
                                        Drive is A:

This means that you have loaded CP/M into the PCW's memory instead of LocoScript, in which case when the disk drive has stopped, remove the disk, and reinsert it in the drive the other way around. Reset the PCW by holding down <SHIFT> and <EXTRA> and then pressing <EXIT>. <EXTRA> is located below the left-hand <SHIFT> key; <EXIT> is located below the right-hand <SHIFT> key. After a few seconds the screen will fill with the main opening display, which is called the *Disk management* menu. This menu has options which enable you to control the files (or documents) stored on your disks and is explained fully in Chapter 2.6.

If you have a PCW8256 with a second drive fitted or a PCW8512, then you should put your copy of LocoScript in Drive A and use Drive B for your data disks. If Amstrad releases a mailmerge program (and a database program) then you will probably need a second drive. If you have a PCW8256 with a single drive and want to run programs like these or others running under CP/M (e.g. the spreadsheet Supercalc2) then you will need two drives (see Appendix B).

2.5 - MAKING COPIES OF DISKS

2.5.1 - Formatting disks

Before a new blank disk can be used it must be formatted. Formatting a disk means creating concentric tracks on its magnetic surface, and dividing the disk into a number of sectors (e.g. like dividing up a cake into equal slices). The PCW's format for Drive A is 40 tracks and 9 sectors (single sided); for Drive B it is 80 tracks and 9 sectors (double sided). Each type of computer has its own particular disk format. These tracks and sectors are invisible to the naked eye; in fact they are made magnetically by the same read/write head that is used to save and load data and programs.

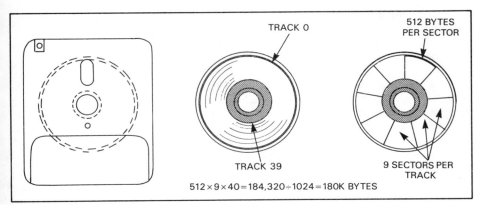

TRACK 0

512 BYTES
PER SECTOR

TRACK 39

9 SECTORS PER
TRACK

512×9×40=184,320÷1024=180K BYTES

Each sector is capable of storing 512 bytes (or characters). As there are 9 sectors per track and 40 tracks that means that each side of a CF2 disk is capable of storing 512×9×40=184,320 bytes. Storage capacity is normally measured in kilobytes (i.e. K); 1 kilobyte = 1024 bytes. Dividing 184,320 by 1024 gives you the CF2's formatted disk capacity of 180K bytes.

CF2-DD disks are capable of storing 512×9×80=368,640 bytes or 360K bytes per side; Drive B uses both sides of the disk hence a CF2-DD's formatted capacity is 720K bytes.

In practice you will find that you can't use all of the 180K (or 720K) for storing your files or documents. 7K is occupied by a directory which is used by LocoScript and CP/M to store the location of the files or documents on each side of the disk; you don't need to worry about how or where your documents and files are stored on a disk as LocoScript and CP/M automatically take care of this for you but it does mean that by the time a directory is added to each side you are left with 173K (or 706K).

In fact a CF2 disk which just has LocoScript on it, and nothing else, leaves just 87K free as LocoScript uses 86K to store its four files. A CF2 disk that doesn't have LocoScript on it, but which can be used to store LocoScript documents, provides the full 173K of storage space. This is known as a data disk and is described more fully in Chapter 2.5.4.

WARNING - The process of formatting a disk totally destroys any data or programs that are present on the disk. Normally you will only want to format new blank disks; you must take great care not to accidentally format your master disks, your working copies or data disks. Pay particular attention to the state of the write protect tabs when formatting disks. As the process of formatting a disk involves writing (recording) on the disk, if the disk is write protected then the formatting program will not work (the disk will not be formatted). Being systematic in the labelling of your disks will help to avoid accidents.

A special utility program, called DISCKIT, is provided to enable you to format disks. Before you can use this utility program you must load the CP/M Plus operating system into the PCW's memory.

To format a disk, check that the drive is empty and switch the PCW on.

Alternatively, if you have already loaded LocoScript into the PCW's memory, then remove and reverse the disk. When you have reinserted it, reset the PCW by holding down <SHIFT> and <EXTRA> and then pressing <EXIT>.

You should see a pattern of black lines begin to fill the screen, and then the following will be displayed:

```
CP/M Plus Amstrad Consumer Electronics plc
vl.4, 61K TPA, 1 disc drive, 112K drive M:
A>_
```

                              Drive is A:

Type DISCKIT in UPPER or lower case letters (do not type DISC KIT) and then press <RETURN>. You should then see something like the following displayed on the screen:

```
                DISC KIT vl.2
              PCW8256 & CP/M Plus
        # 1985 Amstrad Consumer Electronics plc
             and Locomotive Software Ltd
One drive found
Please remove the disc from the drive
Press any key to continue
```

Note that if you press any key with the disk still in the drive, the PCW will display this message again:

```
Please remove the disc from the drive
Press any key to continue
```

So, press any key; you might find pressing the
<SPACE BAR> convenient. The Verify/Format/Copy menu will then
be displayed:

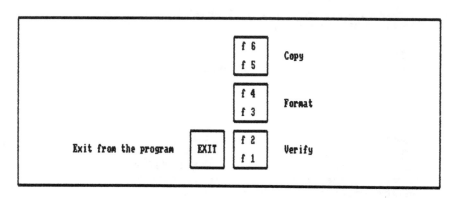

If DISCKIT finds a second drive then you will be asked
which drive (either A or B) will be used for formatting, and
then asked to type Y to confirm that this information has been
typed correctly. Press <f3> to format the disk in Drive A;
press <f1> to format the disk in Drive B. Appropriate
instructions are displayed on the screen at each stage.

If your system has a single drive press <f3> and the
Format menu will be displayed (<f3> is located to the right of
the right-hand <SHIFT> key):

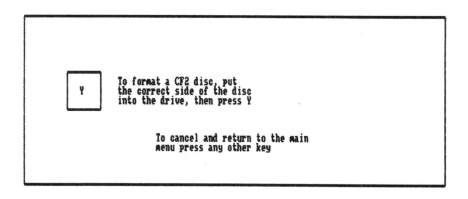

Now insert side 1 (or side A) of the disk that you want
to have formatted. Make sure that it is not write protected. If

you attempt to format a disk that is write protected then the
following message will be displayed:

```
The disc is write protected
Please insert the disc to format into the drive
R-etry or C-ancel?
```

If this message is displayed then press <C> and the
following message will be displayed:

```
Please remove the disc from the drive
Press any key to continue
```

Remove the disk and check that it is the one that you
want to have formatted. Remember that any data or programs on
it will be destroyed when you format it. If you definitely want
to format it, then close the write protect holes so that it is
no longer write protected. You will need to press any key,
before reinserting the disk, in order to invoke the
Verify/Format/Copy menu again. Next, press <f3> to display the
Format menu and then reinsert the disk into the drive.

Note that at this stage, if you press any other key the
display will return to the Verify/Format/Copy menu. The Y may
be typed in UPPER or lower case.

When you have inserted the correct disk to be formatted
and pressed <Y>, the screen will clear and in the top left-hand
corner you will see the number 0 appear which will rapidly be
overwritten by 1, then the 1 will be overwritten by 2, etc.,
until 39 (or 79) has been reached. You might be able to hear
the drive head stepping as it lays down the 40 (or 80) tracks
(0 to 39 = 40; 0 to 79 = 80). Drive A uses 40 track disks (one
side at a time); Drive B uses 80 track disks (both sides).

When the last track has been created the following
message will be displayed on the screen:

```
Format completed
Please remove the disc from the drive
Press any key to continue
```

So remove the disk and press any key (e.g. the

<SPACE BAR>). You will see another Format menu displayed like
this:

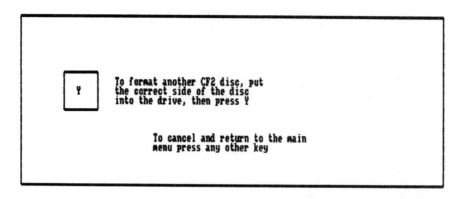

        You will need to format the other side as well, so
reinsert the disk with side 2 (or side B) towards the screen.
Press <Y> to repeat the formatting process.

        When the second side has been formatted remove the disk
and press any key to get back to the Verify/Format/Copy menu.

        It is a good idea to check that the disk has been
formatted correctly so press <f1> to invoke the Verify menu
(<f1> is located to the right of <EXIT>):

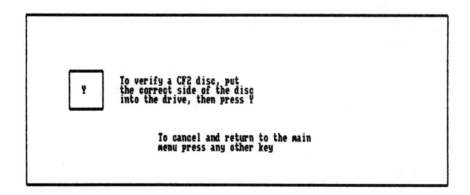

        By now you should be able to follow the instructions on
your own without any difficulty; you should verify both sides
of the disk that has just been formatted.

When you verify a CF2 disk the program will display the following on the screen:

The disc is CF2 format

When the program has finished verifying one side of the disk the following message will be displayed on the screen:

Verify completed
Please remove the disc from the drive
Press any key to continue

When you have verified both sides of the disk press ⟨EXIT⟩ to return to the CP/M prompt A⟩_.

If the PCW ever has a problem reading or writing data on a disk, it will report this in the form of an error message giving you the track and sector numbers in question. You can always establish whether or not the disk is in a good condition by using the verify option, in this menu. If the PCW repeatedly reports an error as occurring in the same track and sector then you should stop using the disk as soon as possible. If you are lucky you might be able to recover some of the files by copying them to another disk.

2.5.2 – How to tell whether or not a disk has been formatted

You can easily check whether or not a disk has been formatted by using the CP/M command DIR; this commands CP/M to display the DIRectory of all the files on the disk. If the disk has not been formatted then CP/M will report an error.

When you have loaded CP/M Plus into the PCW's memory and inserted the disk into the drive, type DIR after the A⟩_ prompt and press ⟨RETURN⟩ like this:

A⟩DIR⟨RETURN⟩

If the PCW finds that the disk is not formatted after a few seconds it will give a single beep and display the following error message at the bottom of the screen:

track 0, sector 0 missing address mark - Retry, Ignore
or Cancel?

This means that it has tried to read the disk and failed. Alternatively, if it reads the disk successfully then a list of the files on the disk will be displayed on the screen.

2.5.3 - Making working copies of your master disks

You will need to make working copies of your master disks in order to safeguard them and to provide disks which can be used for storing your documents. Your master disks should be kept permanently write protected and stored somewhere safe.

Making working copies of your two master disks is quite straightforward. You will need two blank disks. If you haven't got any blank disks then refer back to Chapter 2.1.1. Disks are formatted automatically during the copying process when you use DISCKIT.

Next load CP/M Plus into the PCW. Refer back to Chapter 2.5.1 if you don't recall how to do this. Use the DISCKIT utility which is described in that section and follow the instructions on the screen to invoke the Verify/Format/Copy menu.

When you have the Verify/Format/Copy menu on the screen press <f5> in order to invoke the Copy menu.

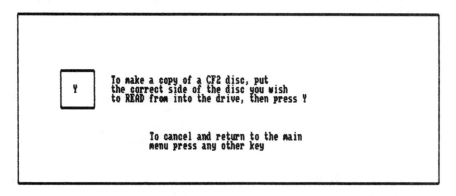

If you are using a PCW8256 fitted with a single drive and want to make a copy of one side of a disk, simply follow the instructions on the screen. You will find that the copying process is carried out in two stages (i.e. tracks 0 to 19 followed by tracks 20 to 39).

However, if you have previously renamed the PROFILE file on your CP/M disk from PROFILE.ENG to PROFILE.SUB, as Amstrad suggest on page 15 of their guide to CP/M in Book 1, then the copying process will be carried out in three stages (i.e. tracks 0 to 13 followed by tracks 14 to 27 and then tracks 28 to 39) because some of the computer's memory that would otherwise be available will have been occupied by the programs that were loaded by the SUBMIT command which is embedded in the file that loads CP/M.

DISCKIT will read some of the data from the source disk (i.e. the disk that you are copying from), and store it temporarily in the PCW's memory. You will then be prompted to remove the source disk and to insert the destination disk (i.e. the disk you are copying to). The data, stored temporarily in the PCW's memory, will then be copied onto the destination disk.

This process of reading, changing disks and then writing will be repeated until all the data has been copied. You will be prompted when to change the disks and told when it is complete. When you copy side 1 (or side A) of a disk be sure to copy to the same side of your destination disk, and not side 2 (or side B), in order to avoid confusion. When copying disks, each side of the source disk is read two (or three) times and so the destination disk must be written to two (or three) times.

If you get confused and mix up the source and destination disks then the program will spot your mistake and warn you with this message:

That is the wrong disk

Even if you mix up the sides of the disk you will still be warned, because each side of the disk is treated as if it is a separate disk. Consequently when this message is displayed it does not necessarily mean that you have inserted the wrong *disk*, but that you have inserted the disk the wrong way around!

If you are using a PCW8256 with a second drive fitted then you might be able to put the source disk in Drive A and the destination disk in Drive B and copy from disk to disk; see Appendix B. Don't forget though that Drive A uses CF2 disks whereas Drive B uses CF2-DD disks.

If you are using a PCW8512 then the copying process will be somewhat simpler because the whole contents of one side of the disk can be read into the computer's memory in one go instead of in several stages. It is possible to have a PCW8256's memory upgraded from 256K to 512K; see Appendix B.

You will need to copy all four sides of your two master disks. When you have done this you should have two disks which are exact copies of your master disks; these are your working

copies. If you *write protect* these disks then they will simply
be backup copies of your *master disks*. If you *write enable*
them then you will be able use them to store your documents.
You might like to keep a set of each.

In order to be able to use the PCW you will need to have
at least one working copy of LocoScript. While you are learning
to use LocoScript with this book you will find it useful to
have a complete copy of the LocoScript disk which Amstrad
supply with the computer.

Eventually you will find it more convenient to use a
working copy of LocoScript which doesn't have all of the
demonstration files on it. You will find that there are some 25
files already on the LocoScript disk which only leaves 46K
free for storing your documents. Any of these demonstration
files can be deleted from the disk, with impunity.

If you want to make a working copy of LocoScript without
the demonstration files on it then you could just make another
copy of the LocoScript *master disk* and then delete all the
demonstration files that you don't want to keep. Alternatively,
you could copy the four LocoScript applications files, which
are required, onto a newly formatted disk. These files are
hidden and are always stored in the first group (i.e. group 0
or LETTERS). If you want to know how to reveal hidden files or
documents then please refer to Chapter 2.7.1.8.

If you are using LocoScript v 1.0 then these files are:

```
J10LOCO.EMS   43K H
JOYCEDIT.JOY  31K H
MAIL232.COM    5K H
MATRIX.STD     7K H
```

If you are using LocoScript v 1.2 then these files are:

```
J20LOCO.EMS   44K H
MAIL232.COM    4K H
MATRIX.STD     7K H
SCRIPT.JOY    31K H
```

So, you should use a complete copy of the LocoScript disk
while you are practising, but create a copy which has just the
four LocoScript files on it for your more serious work.

Because the four LocoScript files take up 86K and you
only need to load LocoScript into the PCW's memory once at the
beginning of the session you might find it useful to have a

disk which has the LocoScript files on one side but not on the
other. Doing this provides an additional 86K in which to store
your documents. A disk like this which doesn't have the four
LocoScript files on it is called a data disk.

2.5.4 - Creating data disks

In addition to your working disks, you will probably need to
create at least one data disk. A data disk can be used by
LocoScript just for storing documents. It doesn't need to
contain the four LocoScript files, as these are usually loaded
into the PCW's memory from your working copy, at the beginning
of each session. Amstrad call this working copy the Start of
Day disk, as it is the first disk that you will use at the
start of each session, to get the PCW up and running.

```
                  Disc management.              Printer idle. Using none.
C=Create new document    E=Edit existing document   P=Print document    D=Direct printing
f1=Disc change   f2=Inspect   f3=Copy   f4=Move  f5=Rename  f6=Erase  f7=Modes  f8=Options
Drive A:                    Drive B:        not fitted   Drive M:
  0k used 173k free   0 files    0k used   0k free   0 files     0k used 102k free    0 files

 group 0    0k    group 4    0k              LETTERS    0k    group 4    0k
 group 1    0k    group 5    0k              SAMPLES    0k    group 5    0k
 group 2    0k    group 6    0k              CONT       0k    group 6    0k
 group 3    0k    group 7    0k              TEMPLATE   0k    group 7    0k
```

You might find it useful to make the reverse side of your
working copy a data disk. That way you can keep one or two
documents that you are working on, on the working copy side
and a lot more documents quite conveniently on the other side.

The simplest way to create a data disk is to format the
side of the disk in question. If you are unsure about how to do
this then please refer to Chapter 2.5.1.

A data disk, therefore, is a disk which has been
formatted, initially doesn't have any files on it and thus
provides you with the full 173K of storage space. That is
approximately 25,000 words or 180 pages of text.

The maximum number of files or documents that you can
store on one side of a disk is 64. When this number has been
reached it will not be possible to save more files even if
there is still some free space remaining on the disk.

If you try adding more you will get an error message
warning that the disk directory is full. One solution would be
to move a document to Drive M, create a new document on the
disk and then merge several documents into it using the *Insert
text* option in the *Editor sub-modes* menu (please see
Chapter 3.2.4.1). Next erase the individual documents from the
disk. Don't forget to move the document on Drive M back to
your disk before switching off or resetting the PCW!
Alternatively, you could move some documents to Drive M, press
<f1> and then move them to another disk.

2.5.5 - Making backup copies of disks

It is standard practice to make backup copies of your
documents on a regular basis, and you are *strongly* advised to
do this.

The frequency with which you copy your documents to your
backup disks and the number of these backup disks, depends on
the type of work that you are doing. For example, if you are
writing a letter to a friend then one backup copy of your
letter on one backup disk should be adequate and, unless you
are of a nervous disposition you will probably be content to
wait until you have finished writing the letter before making
the copy!

However, if you are using the word processor for business
purposes then it would be advisable to keep several backup
disks and to make backup copies of your documents from your
working copy at regular intervals.

It is standard computing practice to keep three copies of
all disks and to label them grandfather/father/son (you might
like to label them grandmother/mother/daughter if you think
your disks are the other gender!). Normally the *son disk* would
be your working disk. The *father disk* would be your first
backup disk and so on.

With the PCW a working copy has less than 87K free (i.e.
about 13,000 words) therefore it makes more sense to use data
disks as your backup disks:

> your first data disk will be your *son disk*
> your second data disk will be your *father disk*
> your third data disk will be your *grandfather disk*

The idea is to copy those documents that you have been
working on, from your working disk to your *son disk* every few

hours. Perhaps more frequently than that depending on what you are doing. You would copy to your *father* disk every day and copy to your *grandfather disk* every week.

You can make a backup copy of a disk by using the copy option of the Copy/Format/Verify menu as described in Chapter 2.5.3. You can also make copies of individual documents or files; this is explained in the next section.

Note that there are two points here:

> the number of backup disks
> the frequency of copying to the backup disks

In the final analysis the frequency with which you backup your work must depend on how long it would take you to re-create it. Accidents do happen all too often, and many a person has lost the contents of a disk only to find that no backup copy exists. Don't take chances; make backup copies of your work regularly.

Backup disks should be kept separate from your working disk. If you value your documents or data then make backup copies as soon as possible and keep them up-to-date. *You have been warned!*

If you are worried about voltage fluctuations in the mains supply or electrical noise on the line then you might want to buy a voltage regulator. Unless you buy an uninterruptable power supply which provides noise suppression then you will still not be protected against a total power failure or something as simple as someone pulling the plug out! The most reliable and cheapest form of protection is to make backup copies regularly.

2.6 - FILE MANAGEMENT

2.6.1 - Disk management menu

The screen always displays the *Disk management* menu whenever you load LocoScript from disk into the PCW's memory, as described in Chapter 2.4.

DISK MANAGEMENT MENU

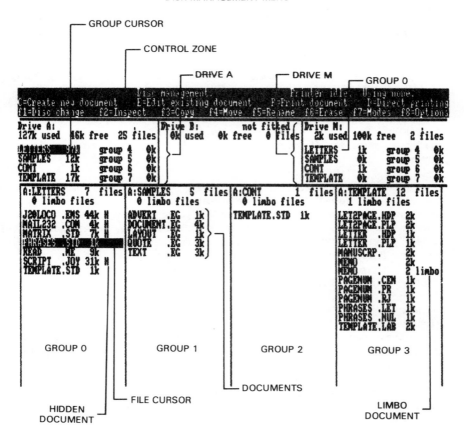

- GROUP CURSOR
- CONTROL ZONE
- DRIVE A
- DRIVE M
- GROUP 0
- GROUP 0
- GROUP 1
- GROUP 2
- GROUP 3
- DOCUMENTS
- HIDDEN DOCUMENT
- FILE CURSOR
- LIMBO DOCUMENT

2.6.1.1 - Control zone

At the top of the screen is a bright section containing three
lines of information which will be referred to as the *Control
zone*. A bright area of the screen like this is called reverse
video. The Control zone stays on the screen all the time you
are using LocoScript, but the information in the Control zone
changes depending on what you are doing. The Control zone also
lets you know what LocoScript is doing and sometimes prompts
you about what to do next.

The Control zone shows you that no drive is in use by
displaying *Using none* in its top line. It is important that you
do NOT attempt to remove a disk when *Using A:* or *Using B:* is
displayed. If *Using none* or *Using M:* (for example while

printing) is displayed, you may change the disk in the drive
with impunity, but you must tell LocoScript immediately after
doing so. You do this by pressing <f1>. You should always
return to the *Disk management* menu before attempting to change
the disk in the drive.

When the word *Printer* is displayed, flashing in the
second line of the Control zone, then LocoScript is reminding
you that the paper bail on the printer has been pulled back
and is waiting just in case you want to make another
adjustment to the printer. Pull the paper loading knob, on the
printer, forwards (towards you) now if you want to see this
happen.

Note that the cursor disappears if you do this while
editing a document. If you are not familiar with the terms
paper bail and paper loading knob, then please refer to the
diagram in Chapter 4. Also note that when the paper bail is
pulled forward, the message displayed in the Control zone is
Printer: Bail bar back. When you push the paper loading knob
towards the back (away from you) the message changes to
Printer: Online Top of form.

As you don't need to make any more adjustments to the
printer you will have to turn this off before you can continue.
Every time the paper loading knob is moved forward the word
Printer is set flashing like this and you will have to stop it,
before you can continue.

You can stop the word *Printer* from flashing by pressing
<EXIT>. Note that the cursor reappears if you do this while
editing a document.

The second line of the Control zone shows you four
options that you can select when LocoScript displays its
Disk management menu:

        C=Create new document –
            enables you to create a brand new document

        E=Edit existing document –
            enables you to make changes to an existing
            document

        P=Print document –
            enables you to print an existing document

        D=Direct printing –
            enables you to use the PCW like an
            electronic typewriter and do direct printing

The first two options are described more fully in Chapter 3.1, the other two are in Chapter 4.3 and Chapter 4.4.

The third line of the Control zone is a menu which offers you a choice of 8 options. For these you use <f1> to <f8>. These are called the function keys. To obtain the even-numbered functions, one of the two <SHIFT> keys must be pressed down when pressing the function key, for example:

        <f1>
        <f2> (i.e. <SHIFT>+<f1>)
        <f3>
        <f4> (i.e. <SHIFT>+<f3>)
        etc.

Try pressing <f1> and you should see the disk drive light come on briefly and *f1=Disc change* in the Control zone, highlighted in reverse video. If you don't feel too confident about experimenting with the other function keys at this stage, don't worry, you really can't do too much harm. Their functions are described more fully in Chapter 2.7.1. If you invoke one of the other pull-down menus accidentally, you can always cancel it by pressing <CAN>.

Notice that when you press any of the function keys, say <f1>, this function alone remains highlighted. Normally, all three lines of the Control zone are highlighted completely.

2.6.1.2 – Drives A, B and M sub-divided into groups 0 to 7

When LocoScript is displaying its *Disk management* menu you will see that below the Control zone there are three boxes. Each box represents a disk drive, hence they are labelled Drive A, Drive B and Drive M.

The Drive A box represents the upper (and in the basic PCW8256 the only) physical disk drive. In the *Disk management* menu this is represented by the left-hand box which shows the name given to the disk in this drive, e.g. *LOCOSCRP.V1*. It shows the amount of disk space already used e.g. *127K used*, the amount of disk space remaining free, e.g. *46K free,* and the number of files on the disk, e.g. *25 files*. It also shows that the disk is divided into 8 *groups* which are numbered from 0 to 7. Amstrad have named the first four of these groups (i.e. groups 0 to 3) LETTERS, SAMPLES, CONT and TEMPLATE. These are arbitrary names and you can rename them if you want to; this is explained more fully in Chapter 2.7.1.5.

The Drive B box represents the second disk drive which is fitted as standard in the PCW8512 but is optional in the PCW8256. In the *Disk management* menu this is represented by the middle box. It is arranged in the same way as Drive A. If you have only one disk drive fitted then the display will be *Drive B: not fitted*.

The Drive M box represents the so-called RAM-disk or Memory disk. This is a section of the PCW's 256K (or 512K) bytes of memory which behaves like another disk. For example, you can copy a file or document from Drive A to Drive M, then change the disk in Drive A and copy it from Drive M to another disk. Chapter 2.7.1.1 and Chapter 2.7.1.3 explains how to do this. It is important to realise that while Drive M can be used as a fast disk drive and thus is very useful, its contents are lost whenever you reset the PCW or switch it off altogether.

You should be able to see an oblong cursor either in Drive A or in Drive M (or in Drive B if you have a second physical drive fitted); this is called the *group* cursor. If you have just loaded LocoScript into the PCW's memory then this cursor will probably be over the LETTERS group (i.e. group 0). You can move this cursor around from group to group within the drives, by pressing either ⟨←⟩, ⟨→⟩, ⟨↑⟩ or ⟨↓⟩, while ⟨SHIFT⟩ is held down. Try doing this now. Notice that sometimes the lower oblong cursor also moves, this is called the *file* cursor and is explained more fully in Chapter 2.6.1.3.

Every LocoScript document that you create must be stored as a separate file in a group in either Drive A or in Drive M (or in Drive B if fitted) and each file must be given a unique description. The file description normally has two parts to it. The first part is called the *filename* and is a specific name, a bit like your first name. The second part of the name is called the *filetype*, is optional and is a generic name a bit like your last name. A full stop (or period) is always used as a separator between the *filename* and the *filetype*.

Filenames can be any combination of up to eight characters and *filetypes* can be any combination of up to three characters. Normally the characters A to Z and 0 to 9 are used; you might find it useful to use # as well. The following characters are not allowed to be used in the name:

         ⟨ ⟩ = ! ¡ * ? & / $ [ ] ( ) . : ; \ + -

So, file descriptions have two parts:

         filename e.g FILENAME
         filetype e.g. TYP

Hence, file description = FILENAME.TYP

Note that even if you type file descriptions in lower case, LocoScript always displays them in UPPER case.

These file descriptions (your documents) are stored in groups; you probably already have groups on your disk called LETTERS, SAMPLES, CONT and TEMPLATE. You are free to rename all 8 groups on either drive, just as you are free to decide which group a file is stored in. If you press <f5> you will see a pull-down menu which enables you to rename files, groups and the disk itself. Press <CAN> as you are not quite ready to make changes like this just yet. This pull-down menu is explained more fully in Chapter 2.7.1.5

Because the final layout of your document is governed by a *template* and because each group has associated with it a particular template, it makes sense to store all your letters in the LETTERS group, all your memos in the MEMO group, etc.

In word processing, a template is like a stencil or a mask that controls where you can place text within a document. Templates are used when you want to ensure that particular documents have standard layouts (or standard formats) hence they are sometimes called standard templates. LocoScript uses special documents as standard templates, to control the layout of ordinary documents. These standard template documents are always called TEMPLATE.STD.

Each drive is divided into 8 groups to help you categorise your documents. For example, you might choose to store all your letters in one group, all your labels in another group, and so on. Each group normally has a standard template of its own. While you might require the letters' standard template to be different from the labels' standard template, LocoScript requires both of them to be called TEMPLATE.STD.

Whenever you create a new document its layout is based on the TEMPLATE.STD held in that group. If you create a document in the LETTERS group then the layout will be that of a letter; if you create a document in the LABELS group then the layout will be that of a label. You would normally keep a standard letter template in the LETTERS group and a standard label template in the LABELS group, etc.

The group called TEMPLATE.STD on the LocoScript disk contains lots of different example templates. If you want to use one of them then you will have to copy it (or move it) to another group and rename the example TEMPLATE.STD. Of course

if there is already a document called TEMPLATE.STD in the
group then you will have to rename the original TEMPLATE.STD
document as something else first (e.g. TEMPLATE.OLD). The three
groups on the LocoScript disk, called LETTERS, SAMPLES and
CONT, already have TEMPLATE.STDs of their own.

Bear in mind that templates are stored just like any
other document because they are documents, albeit special ones;
TEMPLATE.STD documents can be edited just like any other. What
makes a TEMPLATE.STD document special is that its layout
governs the layout of any documents created in that group. The
use of standard templates is explained more fully in
Chapter 3.3.

2.6.1.3 – Groups sub-divided into files (documents)

It is possible to store your documents in any of the eight
groups, in Drive A and/or Drive M (and/or Drive B, if fitted).
Documents can be moved or copied from group to group within a
drive, as well as from a group in one drive to a group in
another drive. You can use the same file description in
different groups, in the same drive, but you can't have two
documents with the same file description in the same group. If
you want to store two documents which have the same file
descriptions in the same group, one of them must be renamed.

Note that you cannot move or copy a document to a group
until that group has been given a name. For example if you try
to copy the file which is called READ.ME from the LETTERS
group in Drive A to group7 the following error message will be
displayed:

> ERROR in: Copy document
> Invalid group name
> ⟩ ◊ Cancel operation ⟨

If this happens just press ⟨ENTER⟩ to select the *Cancel
operation* option.

When LocoScript is loaded into the PCW the group names
from Drive A are copied to Drive M.

Note that the file description READ.ME is actually
displayed as READ   .ME in order to allow for a filename with
a maximum of 8 characters.

To be able to copy (or move) a document in these
circumstances you must first give the group a name using the
rename Group option of the *Rename* menu. Chapter 2.7.1.5
explains how to do this.

Note that if you rename group7 to GROUP7 then LocoScript will accept this as a valid group name and will allow you to copy or move a document to it.

Documents which are stored in any group in Drive A (or Drive B if fitted) will be quite safe, but any documents which are stored in Drive M will be lost when you reset or switch off the PCW. Make sure that you use Drive M as only a temporary storage place; use Drive A (or Drive B if fitted) for the permanent storage of your documents.

If you look at the *Disk management* menu you will see that the *file* cursor normally covers a file description in a column located below one of the drive boxes. The *file* cursor may be moved by means of the cursor control keys ⟨←⟩, ⟨→⟩, ⟨↑⟩ or ⟨↓⟩. Each column represents a group from one of the drives and shows which documents (or files) are stored in that group. If there aren't any files in a group then there won't be a column displayed for it. When you rename a group and create a document in it then LocoScript creates a new column to represent that group.

When you move the *group* cursor to another group in the drive, the *file* cursor automatically moves to the column which represents that group. There are eight columns for each drive but only four of these columns can be displayed on the screen at any given time, so when you try to move the *file* cursor beyond the fourth column the bottom section of the screen moves sideways; this is called panning. When you move the *group* cursor to a group without any documents in it then an empty column is not displayed, but a marker is displayed instead. This marker comprises a pair of vertical lines. The illustration in Chapter 2.5.4 shows one of these markers.

If you create 20 documents in the same group then you will find that as you create the 20th, the column width doubles to accomodate it (each column holds 19 documents). Similarly, when you create the 39th document in a group the column width increases again, and so on. To see this for yourself load LocoScript into the PCW, remove the disk and insert your copy of CP/M and then press ⟨f1⟩.

Files and documents

While information is stored in files on a disk, some files contain programs while others may contain data (e.g. numbers)

or text. LocoScript can produce two different types of text
files:

(1) document files; documents that can be edited

(2) non-document files; files that contain text but
which cannot be edited in the usual way

All documents are files; not all files are documents! For
example, blocks and phrases are stored as non-document files
(see Chapter 3.2.4). In this book, normal document files that
can be edited using LocoScript are called *documents* and
non-document files that cannot be edited in the usual way are
called *files*.

2.7 – DISK HOUSEKEEPING

2.7.1 – *Disk management menu*
(3rd line of Control zone)

If you look at the bottom line of the Control zone you will see
a menu which offers you eight options:

```
f1=Disc change  f2=Inspect  f3=Copy   f4=Move
f5=Rename       f6=Erase    f7=Modes  f8=Options
```

Just press the appropriate function key if you want to
select one of these options, e.g. <f1>. When you press a
function key like this the appropriate option in the Control
zone is highlighted in reverse video. You will find that
pressing some of these keys invokes a pull-down menu, e.g. <f2>
(i.e. <SHIFT>+<f1>). If you press one of these keys in error,
just press <CAN> in order to CANcel the instruction.

2.7.1.1 – f1=Disc change (*Disk management* menu. Control zone)

If you change the disk when LocoScript is displaying its *Disk
management* menu, you must press the <f1> key immediately after
doing so. This lets LocoScript know that the disk has been
changed. If you don't press <f1> and it attempts to access the
disk, then it will detect that the disk has been changed and
display an error message.

For example, assuming that you have only the one physical
drive, Drive A, if you want to make a copy of a document that
is on one disk and store it on another disk, you will have to
copy the document from the source disk (in Drive A) to
Drive M. Next you will have to physically change the disk in

Drive A. Then you will have to copy the document from Drive M
to the destination disk (in Drive A). If you don't press ⟨f1⟩,
after inserting the destination disk, then the following error
message will be displayed:

ERROR in: Copy document
Disc has been changed
⇥ ⬤ Cancel operation   ⇤

If this happens you must press the ⟨ENTER⟩ key in order
to cancel the operation. Doing this also has the same effect as
pressing ⟨f1⟩, so that if you now attempt to copy the document
from Drive M to the disk in Drive A, it will do so without
repeating the error message. Obviously it would be better to
avoid this error message altogether by always pressing the
⟨f1⟩ key after changing a disk in the drive.

Because LocoScript treats each side of the disk as a
separate disk, if it reports that the wrong disk is in the
drive, it may in fact be the correct disk, but the wrong side!
Pressing ⟨f1⟩ in this way applies only to LocoScript and not
to CP/M.

If you press ⟨f1⟩ when using CP/M you will just get ↑Z
displayed on the screen; to let CP/M know that a disk has been
changed press ⟨STOP⟩ (this is equivalent to ↑C which is
sometimes called a warm boot). Unless you will be using CP/M
regularly you don't need to worry about this. However, as you
will be using LocoScript regularly make sure that you do use
the ⟨f1⟩ key!

Note also that you should only change a disk in the drive
when LocoScript is displaying its *Disk management* menu. You
should never change a disk in the drive when LocoScript is
displaying one of its other menus, e.g. creating a new
document, editing an existing document or printing a document.
If you change the disk in Drive A while LocoScript is
displaying its *Edit existing document* menu, and then attempt
to save the document (to the wrong disk) LocoScript will
detect this and report an error:

ERROR in: Drive A:
Disc has been changed
while a document is in use
⇥ ⬤ Retry operation   ⇤
Cancel operation
Ignore error and continue

If this happens, remove the disk, reinsert the correct disk, and then press the <ENTER> key in order to select the *Retry operation* option. The <f1> key serves a different purpose when LocoScript is displaying its *Edit existing document* menu.

2.7.1.2 - f2=Inspect (*Disk management* menu. Control zone)

When you load LocoScript from your working copy of the LocoScript master disk, you will see that Amstrad have named group 1, SAMPLES. Note that the groups are numbered from 0 to 7 so group 1 is the second group. If you move the *file* cursor so that it is over the document which is called DOCUMENT.EG and press the <f2> key (i.e. <SHIFT>+<f1>) you should see a pull-down menu like this displayed:

```
          ⅋ Inspect document  ⅌
            Name: DOCUMENT.EG
            Group: SAMPLES
            Drive: A
            Sample Document
            Software for CP/M on PCW8256
            used to illustrate pagination
```

After you have been using LocoScript for a while you will find that your disk begins to fill up with the documents that you have saved. You will probably find that the eight characters provided for the *filename* and three characters for the *filetype* are not enough.

LocoScript allows you to store a short piece of text or summary which is called an Identity, and that describes your document more fully. You will find this feature useful if you take the trouble to use it. You can use it to check on a document's identity without having to load the document into the computer's memory. Apart from editing a document the only other way of being able to see a document is to print it.

Note that the top line of the menu is a cursor. You can change the Name, Group and/or Drive by moving the *menu* cursor down using the <↓> key.

If you want to set up or change the Identity text, this has to be done while editing the document with LocoScript displaying its *Edit existing document* menu. Invoke the *Modes* menu by selecting the f7=Modes option from the third line of the Control zone. Then select the *Edit Identify text* option from this menu by moving the cursor down (press <↓> once) and pressing <ENTER>.

LocoScript allows you to store three lines of thirty characters. You will see a *menu* cursor displayed in the first line and the remaining two lines displayed in reverse video. The *menu* cursor can be moved down and back up by means of the ⟨↓⟩ and ⟨↑⟩ keys.

You will find that a *character* cursor appears within the *menu* cursor when you type a character, press the space bar, press ⟨→⟩ or ⟨←⟩. You can use the ⟨DEL→⟩ and ⟨←DEL⟩ keys to delete existing text on a line and use ⟨→⟩ and ⟨←⟩ to move the *character* cursor along the line. If you want to type in more than thirty characters you will have to move the *menu* cursor down to the second line, and so on.

Note that unless you make an effort to alter it, the document's identity will be the same as that in the group's TEMPLATE.STD, because whenever you create a document it is based on the group's TEMPLATE.STD and therefore inherits its characteristics, including its identity.

If you want to practise using the Identity facility you will find it useful to spend some time looking at the Identities of each of the sample templates that Amstrad have supplied. The TEMPLATE group contains lots of useful templates; this is explained more fully in Chapter 3.3.1.

2.7.1.3 − f3=Copy (*Disk management* menu. Control zone)

LocoScript allows you to copy documents from one group to another and from drive to drive. Copying a document or file causes a new copy to be created while keeping the original intact.

You might like to try copying a document now; make sure that you use your working copy of LocoScript and that it is not write protected. If you are unsure about this point then please refer to Chapter 2.1.4.

Copying documents from one group to another

Imagine that you need to copy the document called ADVERT.EG from the group called SAMPLES, to the group called CONT, and name the new document JUNK.007. This is how you would do it.

When LocoScript is displaying its *Disk management* menu, move the *group* cursor to cover the group called SAMPLES, move the *file* cursor to cover the document called ADVERT.EG and then press ⟨f3⟩. Doing this highlights the f3=Copy option in the

third line of the Control zone. Press <ENTER> to invoke a
pull-down menu like this:

```
Copy document
 ⇥ New Name: ?          ,      ⇤
   Group:    SAMPLES
   Drive:    A
   Old Name: ADVERT   .EG
   Group:    SAMPLES
   Drive:    A
```

If the menu that is displayed doesn't look like this, then
press <CAN> and start again. Alternatively, you could move the
cursor down, using <↓>, and change either of the groups, drives
or the old name.

LocoScript will automatically make the name of the
destination (new) group the same as the source (old) group and
the destination drive the same as the source drive. It tries to
save you the effort of typing unnecessarily, by assuming that
the destination group and drive are going to be the same as
those of the source.

You will have to type in the new file description
(i.e. JUNK.007). When you have typed the *filename* JUNK (you
can use <←DEL> to correct any mistake you make) press <.> or
the <SPACE BAR> once and then type in the *filetype 007*. Note
that you don't have to type the full stop (or period), if you
press the space bar; LocoScript puts it in for you
automatically, together with the four spaces.

The *menu* cursor can be moved down or back up using <↓>
and <↑>. Now press <↓> to move the cursor down one line.

To copy the file from the group called SAMPLES to the
group called CONT you will need to change the group name.
Slowly type CONT, and notice that the group name ends up as
CONTLES! Press the <SPACE BAR> once and the group name will
change to CONT. When the menu looks like this press <ENTER>
and you should see the disk drive indicator lamp glow brightly
and *Using A:* displayed in the Control zone.

```
Copy document
   New Name: JUNK     .007
 ⇥ Group:    CONT          ⇤
   Drive:    A
   Old Name: ADVERT   .EG
   Group:    SAMPLES
   Drive:    A
```

After a few seconds you will see your JUNK.007 file appear in the CONT group, in Drive A. Notice that the original file ADVERT.BG is still in the SAMPLES group.

If you want to retain the same document name you don't have to type it, just position the *file* cursor over the document and press <f3>, then move the *file* cursor to the destination group (any drive) and press <ENTER> twice. You can use the same shortcut when moving documents.

Error messages

If you make a mistake when typing the file description (e.g. if you leave the new file description blank or type the new file description incorrectly) then LocoScript will display an error message like this:

```
    ERROR in: Copy document
    Invalid file name
→ ● Cancel operation            ←
```

Press <ENTER> in order to return to the *Disk management* menu.

Similarly, if you make a mistake in typing the group name (e.g. if you type a name that doesn't exist) then LocoScript will display another error message:

```
    ERROR in: Copy document
    Invalid group name
→ ● Cancel operation            ←
```

Press <ENTER> in order to return to the *Disk management* menu.

Copying documents from one disk to another via Drive M

If you want to copy a document from a disk in Drive A (or Drive B) to Drive M in order to be able to copy it from Drive M to another disk, then you MUST tell LocoScript that you have changed the disk, by pressing <f1>, between inserting the destination disk and attempting to copy the document from Drive M to Drive A (or Drive B).

If you don't press <f1> then LocoScript will display an error message warning that the disk has been changed and inviting you to cancel the operation. If this happens then press <ENTER>.

For example, imagine that you want to copy the document called READ.ME from your working copy of LocoScript to the same group on another disk. Assuming that your working copy is already in Drive A, and that there is a group called LETTERS in Drive M and on the other disk, then this is how you would do it:

Move *group* cursor to Drive A: LETTERS group
Move *file* cursor to READ.ME document
Press <f3> and then <ENTER> to invoke copy menu
Type in the new name READ.ME
Type in the new Drive: M
Press <ENTER> to copy READ.ME to Drive M

Remove the source disk
Insert the destination disk
Press <f1> to inform LocoScript of disk change

Move *group* cursor to Drive M: LETTERS group
Move *file* cursor to READ.ME document
Press <f3> and then <ENTER> to invoke copy menu
Type in the new name READ.ME
Type in the new Drive: A
Press <ENTER> to copy READ.ME to Drive A

Note that LocoScript will not allow you to copy a document to a group which hasn't been named (e.g. group7).

2.7.1.4 – f4=Move (*Disk management* menu. Control zone)

LocoScript allows you to move documents from one group to another and from drive to drive. Moving a document or file causes it to be transferred from one location to another; the original is lost. Note that the operations used for moving documents are almost identical to those used for copying documents. You might like to try moving a document now.

Moving from group to group

Imagine that you need to move ADVERT.EG from the group called SAMPLES, to the group called CONT, and at the same time rename the document as LAWNMOWR.AD1, then this is how you would do it.

Move the *group* cursor to the SAMPLES group, move the *file*
cursor to ADVERT.EG and then press <f4> (i.e. <SHIFT>+<f3>).
Press <ENTER> to invoke a pull-down menu like this:

```
Move document
⇒ New Name: ?          ,        ⇐
   Group:   SAMPLES
   Drive:   A
   Old Name: ADVERT   .EG
   Group:   SAMPLES
   Drive:   A
```

You will have to type in LAWNMOWR.AD1. When you have
typed LAWNMOWR (take care not to type LAWNMOWER; you can use
the <←DEL> key to correct any mistake you make) type AD1. Note
that you don't have to type the full stop; LocoScript puts it
in for you automatically.

```
Move document
   New Name: LAWNMOWR.AD1
⇒ Group:   CONT          ⇐
   Drive:   A
   Old Name: ADVERT   .EG
   Group:   SAMPLES
   Drive:   A
```

After a few seconds you will see LAWNMOWR.AD1 appear in
the CONT group, in Drive A. Notice that the original document
ADVERT.EG has disappeared from the SAMPLES group.

If you want to move the document called LAWNMOWR.AD1
from the group called CONT, back to SAMPLES, and rename it
ADVERT.EG. This is how you would do it.

Move the *group* cursor to CONT, move the *file* cursor to
LAWNMOWR.AD1 and then press <f4> (i.e. <SHIFT>+<f3>). Press
<ENTER> to invoke a pull-down menu like this:

```
Move document
⇒ New Name: ?          ,        ⇐
   Group:   CONT
   Drive:   A
   Old Name: LAWNMOWR.AD1
   Group:   CONT
   Drive:   A
```

Type in the original file description (i.e. ADVERT.EG).
and change the group name from CONT to SAMPLES. When the menu
looks like this press <ENTER>.

```
Move document
New Name: ADVERT  .EG
⇥ Group:   SAMPLES        ⇤
Drive:    A
Old Name: LAWNMOWR.AD1
Group:    CONT
Drive:    A
```

After a few seconds you will see ADVERT.EG file reappear
in the SAMPLES group, in Drive A.

Error messages

If you make a mistake typing the file description or group
name then LocoScript will warn you with an appropriate error
message (similar to those shown in Chapter 2.7.1.3).

Moving documents from one drive to another via Drive M

As with copying, if you want to move a document from Drive A
(or Drive B) to Drive M in order to move it from Drive M to
another disk then you MUST tell LocoScript that you have
changed the disk, by pressing <f1>, between inserting the
destination disk and attempting to move the document from
Drive M to Drive A (or Drive B).

Note that LocoScript will not allow you to move a
document to a group which hasn't been named (e.g. group 7).

Make sure that you check that all documents/files in
Drive M have been copied/moved to Drive A (or Drive B) before
switching off or resetting the machine.

2.7.1.5 - f5=Rename (*Disk management* menu. Control zone)

Pressing <f5> invokes the *Rename* menu which looks like this:

```
⇥ 0 rename document    ⇤
    recover from Limbo
    rename Group
    rename Disc
```

Note that the *menu* cursor can be moved down and back up
using <↓> and <↑>. To select an option move the cursor so that
it covers your choice and then press <ENTER>.

Renaming a document

If you select the *rename document* option then a pull-down menu will be displayed, for example like this:

```
rename document
⇥ New Name  ?              ⇤
  Old Name: ADVERT  .EG
  Group:    SAMPLES
  Drive:    A
```

To change the document from ADVERT.EG to LAWNMOWR.AD1 type LAWNMOWRAD1 (without typing the full stop (or period)) and press <ENTER>. To change ADVERT.EG to AD just type AD and press <ENTER>. Remember that a file description has two parts to it:

```
file description = FILENAME.TYP
filename = maximum 8 characters
filetype = maximum 3 characters (optional)
```

This is described more fully in Chapter 2.6.1.2.

Renaming a group

If you select the *rename Group* option then a pull-down menu will be displayed, for example like this:

```
rename Group
⇥ New Name  ?          ⇤
  Group:    SAMPLES
  Drive:    A
```

To change the Group name from SAMPLES to FREEBIES just type FREEBIES and press <ENTER>. You are limited to eight characters the first of which must be a letter.

Renaming a disk

If you select the *rename Disk* option then a pull-down menu will be displayed, for example like this:

```
rename Disc
⇥ New Name  ?          .      ⇤
  Drive:    A
```

To change the Disk name from LOCOSCRP.V1 to WORKNG#A.CPY just type the new name and press <ENTER>. The restrictions that apply to the file description also apply to the Disk name.

If your disk is write protected, LocoScript will detect
this and tell you:

```
        Error in: rename (document/group/drive)
        Disc is write protected
   ⅋ ● Cancel operation ⅌
        Disc write enabled; continue
```

Either press <ENTER>, to cancel the operation or if you
want to continue, remove the disk from the drive, write enable
it, reinsert it and press <↓> followed by <ENTER>.

2.7.1.6 – f6=Erase (Disk management menu. Control zone)

Erasing documents

This option enables you to erase documents (or delete files)
from your disks. To invoke the Erase document menu press <f6>
(i.e. <SHIFT>+<f5>).

```
        Erase document
     ⅋ Name:  ?                ⅌
       Group:
       Drive:
```

If you position the file cursor over the document that
you want to erase you will find that LocoScript inserts the
Name, Group and Drive information automatically for you.

For example, if you want to erase the document called
ADVERT.EG just position the file cursor over it and press
<ENTER>.

```
        Erase document
     ⅋ Name:  ADVERT  .EG ⅌
       Group: SAMPLES
       Drive: A
```

If you position the cursor over the wrong file then press
<CAN> to quit the Erase document menu.

Putting documents into Limbo

Whenever you erase a document in this way LocoScript places it
in a state of Limbo, where it will be held providing there is
enough space for it. If you don't bother to restore the
document then eventually it will be deleted permanently (when
there is no longer enough space to store it). How long it

remains in *Limbo* for depends on the amount of remaining free space on your disk. When you save a document on disk, LocoScript will delete a *Limbo* file permanently if it has to, in order to make room for the new document.

If you feel that leaving copies of documents in Limbo presents a security risk then you can permanently erase a document from a disk altogether by erasing the Limbo version after erasing the document.

Chapter 2.7.1.8 explains how to get LocoScript to display the names of any Limbo documents.

Recovering documents from Limbo

If you want to recover a Limbo file then set a tick against the *Limbo* option as described above, and position the *file* cursor over the *Limbo* file. Press <f5> to invoke the *Rename* menu. Move the *menu* cursor down to the *recover from Limbo* option, using <↓> and press <ENTER>. Doing this invokes a pull-down menu. Here is an example of what you would see if you were trying to recover a document called COMEBACK.NOW!

```
    recover from Limbo
  ↱ New Name: COMEBACK.NOW ↰
    Old Name: COMEBACK.NOW
    Group:    LETTERS Limbo
    Drive:    A
```

The document will be restored by pressing <ENTER>, provided that there isn't already a document with the same name in the group.

If the file description already exists then you will have to rename the existing document before you can recover the Limbo document.

2.7.1.7 - f7=Modes (*Disk management* menu. Control zone)

This option enables you to run other software from LocoScript. For example, you might want to run a mail-merge program; please refer to the Glossary if you are not familiar with this term.

If you press <f7> you will see a pull-down menu like this displayed:

```
         Select mode
  ⇥ ● Edit document    ⇤
     Print document
     Create document
     Direct printing
     Make ASCII file
```

The *Edit document* option is exactly the same as the *Edit existing document* option that is displayed in the *Disk management* menu Control zone.

The *Print document*, *Create document*, and *Direct printing* options are also exactly the same as their equivalents in the *Disk management* menu Control zone.

The *Edit* and *Create* options are described in more detail in Chapter 3.1. The other two are described in Chapter 4.3 and Chapter 4.4.

If you select the *Make ASCII file* option then you will see *Making ASCII file, Pick destination Group and Drive using cursor keys, then press ENTER, or CANCEL to abandon* displayed in the Control zone. Also a pull-down menu similar to this will be displayed:

```
         Make ASCII file
  ⇥ New Name: ?             ⇤
     Group: LETTERS
     Drive: A
     Old Name: Document.000
     Group: LETTERS
     Drive: A
  ● Simple text file
     Page image file
```

The tick can be moved from *Simple text file* to *Page image file* using <↓>.

Before LocoScript documents can be used by other programs the special codes which control the way the text is displayed and printed have to be removed. These options are used for that purpose.

Computers can't store letters, they can only store numbers, so the keyboard characters you type are converted into a number code which is called ASCII. A file which only contains ASCII codes can be used by other programs, files which contain the special embedded control codes cannot.

LocoScript enables you to make either a *simple text* file or a *page image* file. In either case the file just contains ASCII codes (no embedded control codes).

While a simple text file doesn't include any layout information it does include TABs and carriage RETURNS. This is the most basic type of text file.

A page image file is a simple text file that contains additional spaces in order to retain the layout (the line breaks are the same). If a word is broken then a hyphen is inserted. The ASCII code for a form feed (new page) is inserted at the bottom of each page.

Typically you might use this feature to convert LocoScript documents into a form that can be passed to another printer or passed to another computer via a modem (given the CPS8256 Centronics Parallel/Serial interface option; see Chapter 5.1.1.4), or passed to another program running under CP/M.

If you create simple text or page image files it is a good idea to label them clearly as non-LocoScript documents. For example make the *filetype* ASC. Alternatively copy them to another disk to avoid confusion.

Have a look at the document called READ.ME on your master disk where you will find a section which explains the use of ASCII files more fully. Also, if you read page 29 of the CP/M Plus section in Amstrad's Book 1, you will see that it is possible to edit ASCII files using CP/M.

If you want to import an ASCII file into LocoScript first create a new document in the usual way, then press <f7> and select the *Insert text* option. Doing this takes you out of the document that you have created to the *Disk management* menu. Move the file cursor over the ASCII file and press <ENTER> twice. The file will then be inserted in your document. If you want to stop it at any time press <STOP>. If you want to stop it permanently press <STOP> again, otherwise press any other key.

2.7.1.8 - f8=Options (*Disk management* menu. Control zone)

Normally both *Limbo* and *Hidden* documents are not displayed. If you want all *Limbo* or all *Hidden* documents to be displayed in

the *Disk maintenance* menu, then you will need to *set* a tick
against the appropriate option in the *Modes* menu. If you press
<f8> (i.e. <SHIFT>+<f7>) the *Show options* menu will be
displayed like this:

> Show options
> ⇒ Limbo   ⇐
>   Hidden

You can use <[+]> to *set* a tick against the *Limbo* and/or
Hidden options. Press <↓> to move the *menu* cursor down to the
Hidden option and press <[+]>.

> Show options
>   Limbo
> ⇒ Hidden   ⊕ ⇐

Note that LocoScript automatically hides the *Hidden*
documents and any *Limbo* documents each time you load
LocoScript back into the PCW's memory, unless you tell it to do
otherwise.

SUMMARY

- At present the 5¼-inch disk is the industry standard
  size; the 3-inch and 3½-disks are becoming increasingly
  popular.
- The 3-inch CF2 (or CF-2) disks have their sides labelled
  A (or 1) and B (or 2).
- Both sides of a disk can be used for storing programs or
  data but Drive A can only read one side of a disk at a
  time.
- When a write protect hole is open that side of the disk
  is *write protected*.
- When a write protect hole is closed that side of the disk
  is *write enabled*.
- Programs or data stored in Drive M, are lost when the PCW
  is switched off.
- LocoScript makes extensive use of pull-down menus. A
  pull-down menu can be cancelled by pressing <CAN>.
- Some menus contain a *menu* cursor which can be moved
  using the cursor control keys <↑>, <→>, <↓> and <←>.
  ⇒ Represents a *menu* cursor ⇐.
- Sometimes a tick is displayed to indicate the current
  choice in a menu. In some menus this tick can be toggled
  on or off by means of <[+]> and <[-]>. ⊕ is used to
  represent a tick.
- The master disks contain the programs which make the PCW
  work.

- You should be using LocoScript version 1.2 (at least).
- Make sure that you use your working copies and NOT the master disks on a day-to-day basis.
- A disk which just has LocoScript on it leaves 87K free. A data disk leaves 173K free.
- Formatting a disk totally destroys all programs and/or data stored on it.
- The special utility program called DISCKIT which is provided to enable you to format, verify and copy disks cannot be used until you have loaded CP/M Plus into the PCW's memory.
- To reset the PCW hold down <SHIFT>+<EXTRA> and press <EXIT>.
- Make backup copies of your disks; update your backup copies regularly.
- To stop *Printer* from flashing in the Control zone press <EXIT>.
- If you accidentally invoke a pull-down menu press <CAN>.
- Drives A and B are the upper and lower physical drives. Drive M is the memory disk.
- The *Disk management* menu has two oblong cursors called the *group* and *file* cursors.
- A file description has two parts; the *filename* (maximum 8 characters) is separated from the *filetype* (maximum 3 characters) by a full stop (or period).
- Each drive is divided into 8 groups numbered from 0 to 7.
- Whenever you create a new document its layout is determined by the TEMPLATE.STD document held in that group.
- You cannot copy (or move) a document to a group which hasn't been named.
- If you change a disk you must press <f1> after inserting the new disk.
- LocoScript allows you to store a short piece of text or summary which is called an Identity.
- Copying a document creates a new copy and keeps the original intact.
- Moving a document transfers it from one location to another; the original is lost.
- Whenever you erase a document, LocoScript places it in a state of *Limbo*.
- Normally any *Limbo* and all *Hidden* documents are not displayed in the *Disk management* menu.
- Characters typed from the keyboard are converted by the computer into a number code called ASCII.

3   LocoScript, the Word Processor

LocoScript makes extensive use of menus, particularly pull-down menus, to provide you with on-screen help. A pull-down menu is like a roller blind with a number of options written on it. To pull down or invoke a menu, you need to press one of the PCW's dedicated word-processing keys. These pull-down menus are very helpful, particularly when LocoScript is new to you, but you will soon find yourself taking the various short-cuts which LocoScript provides to enable you to miss out many of the menus, as you gain confidence in using the word processor. See Chapter 3.5 which is entitled BY-PASSING MENUS.

Note that you must use <ENTER> to pass your instructions to LocoScript and that <RETURN> cannot be used for this purpose. <RETURN> is equivalent to the carriage return key on an electric typewriter and means end the line here. <SHIFT LOCK> also works just like that on a typewriter. Locking <SHIFT LOCK> on causes the UPPER case characters to be produced. When <SHIFT LOCK> is locked on, a small light in the key itself is illuminated; pressing it again or either of the <SHIFT> keys turns <SHIFT LOCK> (and its light) off. In fact, the keyboard uses the standard QWERTY layout, except for some special-purpose keys which are dedicated to word processing and are located mainly at the right-hand end.

LocoScript uses various cursors to point at particular parts of the screen. A cursor is an oblong shape which sometimes also highlighted in reverse video and sometimes is displayed flashing:

the *group* cursor is the upper oblong which is displayed in the *Disk management* menu, it is highlighted and does not flash.

the *file* cursor is the lower oblong which is displayed in the *Disk management* menu, it is highlighted and does not flash.

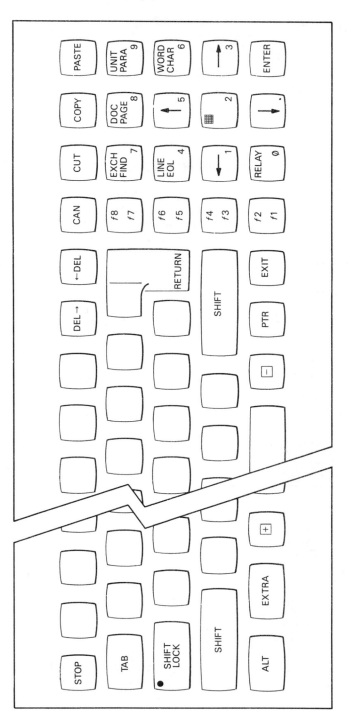

THE PCW's KEYBOARD SHOWING THE KEYS DEDICATED TO WORD PROCESSING

menu cursors indicate an option which can be selected; generally they are not highlighted and do not flash.

the *character* cursor is small, highlighted and flashes except when it is used within *menu* cursors.

3.1 — USING LOCOSCRIPT FOR THE FIRST TIME

The purpose of this section is to introduce you to the main word processing operations. Chapter 3.2 contains an introduction to the word processing facilities which will enable you to manipulate the text in a document.

If you look at the Control zone in the *Disk management* menu you will see that the second line is really a menu with four options:

```
C=Create new document  E=Edit existing document
P=Print document       D=Direct printing
```

Each of these options represents a different word processing operation.

3.1.1 — C=Create new document (*Disk management* menu option)

If you want to create a brand new document then you will need to use this option. Position the *group* cursor in the LETTERS group and press <C>, then a pull-down menu like this will appear on the screen:

```
 Create document
⇥ Name:  DOCUMENT.000 ⇤
  Group: LETTERS
  Drive: A
```

Notice LocoScript suggests that you use the name DOCUMENT.000 for your new document. You don't have to accept this if you don't want to; you can type in a name of your own if you prefer. If you decide to accept the suggested name, when you come to create another document LocoScript will suggest that you use DOCUMENT.001, and so on. Note that there is a cursor in this menu which can be moved down and back up using <↓> and <↑>. You can also change the group or drive if you want to.

IMPORTANT - Whenever you create a new document in a group, it inherits its layout characteristics from the group's standard template (i.e. TEMPLATE.STD). The TEMPLATE.STD document determines the layout of every new document created in that group. While any document's layout can be changed later by editing the header, obviously if you make the wrong choice at this stage it will cause you unnecessary work later. If you plan to create a number of new documents in the same group then you would be wise to check the details of that group's TEMPLATE.STD, just in case it needs changing. If you want to alter a TEMPLATE.STD then please refer to Chapter 3.3.

When you are happy with the file description, group and drive, press <ENTER> and LocoScript will change from displaying its *Disk management* menu to displaying its *Editing text* menu. You should then see something like this at the top of the screen:

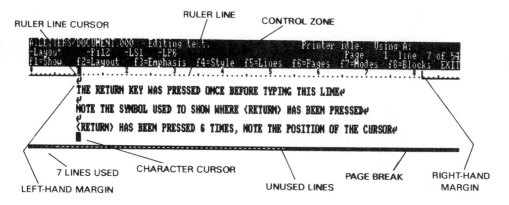

Immediately below the Control zone you will see a dotted line (with some numbers above it) which extends across the screen this is called the *ruler line*; it has solid lines at either end which represent the left-hand and right-hand margins. It is unlikely that what you see will be exactly the same as this, because it depends on the TEMPLATE.STD that you are using. For example, the left and right-hand margins will probably be different. Notice that there is a cursor in the ruler line which is separate from the *character* cursor itself. The *ruler line* cursor follows the *character* cursor as you move it left and right using <←> and <→>, but it always remains in the ruler line; use it to ascertain the lateral position of the *character* cursor. Also, see Chapter 3.3.2.

The line which extends across the screen is the page break. If you look at it closely you will see that it actually comprises three horizontal lines. Its middle line acts as an indicator showing you how many lines on the page have been used and how many remain unused. The bright dashes at the left-hand end indicate the number of remaining lines on the page. The dark dashes in the middle indicate the number of lines remaining unused. The right-hand end of this middle line is not used; its length depends on the number of lines on the page. Each time you use up a line by pressing <RETURN> you will see one of these dark dashes change into a bright dash. By this means you can always see how many lines of the page remain unused.

If you want to check how many lines in a page have been used you will need to be able to see all of the dashes in the page break so the 0 in the ruler line must be displayed on the screen. If you hold down <←> for a few seconds, the cursor will move to the left-hand end of the screen (the text might move to the right).

You will find that LocoScript allows documents which are wider than the screen to be created; the ruler line extends from 0 to just over 25 units, whereas the screen has only a width of 9 ruler line units. Note that the printer limits you to 80 columns.

Alternatively, the length of the page (a number of lines) and the *character* cursor's vertical position on the screen (its line number) are always displayed in the Control zone. For example, *line 18 of 47*.

Notice that the *character* cursor moves to the right as you type in letters and spaces; it shows you exactly where you are on the screen. If you make a mistake and type the wrong letter, you can delete your mistake using <←DEL>. This key is located above <RETURN>.

> <←DEL> deletes the character to the left of the cursor (it also moves the *character* cursor one character to the left; watch the *ruler line* cursor).

When you type in text which is longer than one line, LocoScript puts in the carriage return for you automatically. This is called wraparound or word wrap.

> <←> moves the cursor left one character
> <→> moves the cursor right one character
> <←DEL> deletes the character to the left of the cursor

⟨DEL→⟩ deletes the character that the cursor is on (and causes all the remaining characters in the line to move one character to the left)
⟨↑⟩ moves the cursor up one line
⟨↓⟩ moves the cursor down one line

You can only use ⟨↓⟩ and ⟨↑⟩ if you have typed in more than one line. Also, if you hold down any of these keys for more than about a second their function is repeated. In fact the same applies to the other characters of the keyboard. Try holding down ⟨A⟩ for a few seconds.

LocoScript always displays your text on the screen (in terms of line endings) the way it will be printed. What you see is what you get (WYSIWYG)!

If you press ⟨EXIT⟩ you will see a pull-down menu like this displayed:

Exit options:
↯ ✪ Finish editing   ⇐
    Save and Continue
    Save and Print
    Abandon edit

3.1.1.1 – Finish editing option (*Exit options* menu option)

If you press ⟨ENTER⟩ LocoScript will assume that you have finished working on the document for now and save it using the drive that you selected when you pressed ⟨C⟩ to create the document.

Note that if the drive selected was M then you will lose the document when you next switch off or reset the PCW. If you want to prevent this happening make sure that you move the document from Drive M to either Drive A or B, as soon as LocoScript has returned to its *Disk management* menu.

3.1.1.2 – Save and Continue option (*Exit options* menu option)

The *Edit option* menu has a cursor which can be moved down and back up using ⟨↓⟩ and ⟨↑⟩. When you move the *menu* cursor down the tick moves with it.

If you select the Save and Continue option then LocoScript will save the document, as described above, but remain in its *Editing text* menu. Unfortunately, it returns the *character* cursor to the top of the document and not to where you left it. To get around this problem place a *UniT* marker in

the text before you select this option. Then when LocoScript
has finished saving the document move the *character* cursor to
the *UniT* marker by pressing <UNIT>. When LocoScript has moved
the cursor to *the UniT* marker, delete it. The use of the *UniT*
marker is described in more detail in Chapter 3.2.2.

LocoScript constantly formats your document for the
printer while it is being edited, sometimes this can be a
painfully slow process particularly when it comes to saving a
long document. You will probably find that you need to limit
your documents to about 40K; anything over that size becomes
rather cumbersome.

It takes about one minute for each 10K of document saved,
so saving a long document, if the cursor is at the top, calls
for some patience. Once formatted the document is sent to the
disk in a print ready state, which means that you can be
printing one document while editing another. Not all
microcomputers will allow you to work this way, indeed some
costing considerably more than your PCW will force you wait
while printing. With the PCW the delay occurs when you save a
document, with other machines the delay occurs during printing,
either way there is a delay. Nevertheless, using a word
processor is still a lot faster than typing, especially when
you consider all the other clever things the PCW can do.

In fact LocoScript can do some things that other more
expensive word processors can't do, so if you have used another
word processor before you might be pleasantly surprised at
what you find. Alternatively, if this is the first time that you
have used a word processor, 'you ain't seen nothing yet'!

If you find the delay during saving a nuisance you can
always use the <[≡]> key (i.e. between <←> and <→>) as an alarm
to indicate when LocoScript has reached the end of a long
process like this. Press <[≡]> after starting the lengthy
process. When LocoScript is ready to receive its next
instruction it will give a loud 'beep'.

3.1.1.3 – Save and Print option (*Exit options* menu option)

Make sure that you set up the printer properly before selecting
this option. The procedure for setting up the printer is
described in Chapter 4.

If you select this option LocoScript will first save the
document, just as if you had selected the *Finish editing*
option, and then print the whole document. If you only want to

print part of the document select the *Finish editing* option from the *Edit options* menu and then select the *P=Print document* option from the *Disk management* menu. Chapter 4 explains how to use this menu to print selected pages of a document.

3.1.1.4 - Abandon edit (*Exit options* menu option)

If you select this option then LocoScript will assume that you do not want to keep the document and will destroy it permanently. Note that it does NOT put it into a state of Limbo. For an example see Chapter 3.2.1.2.

3.1.2 - E=Edit existing document (*Disk management* menu option)

This option enables you to edit an existing document which has already been saved using one of the drives. You can use this option to make changes to the document or just to add more text to it. If you want to edit a document, move the *group* cursor to the appropriate drive so that it covers the group that your document is located in and then move the *file* cursor over the document that you want to edit.

When you press <E>, a pull-down menu will display the file description, group and drive of the current document. Pressing <ENTER> causes LocoScript to change from displaying the *Disk management* menu to displaying the *Edit text* menu and the top of the current document to be displayed on the screen. When you see the *character* cursor flashing at the top of the screen you know that LocoScript is ready for you to start amending the document.

When you have finished editing the document you can return to the *Disk maintenance* menu as described in Chapter 2.6.1. The only difference is that if you use the *Abandon edit* option LocoScript only destroys the current version that you are working on. The original version will be remain unaffected.

If you attempt to change the disk in the drive while editing LocoScript will report an error:

```
        Error in: Drive A
        Disc has been changed
        while document is in use
    ⇥ ⊕ Retry operation ⇤
        Cancel operation
        Ignore error and continue
```

Replace the original disk in the drive and press <ENTER>.
Do NOT ignore the error.

3.1.2.1 - Making space for your document while editing

Before it allows you to edit a document LocoScript creates a
backup copy of the document just in case you decide to abandon
the edit and want to revert to the original copy. If for some
reason LocoScript was unable to save the edited version and
hadn't kept a copy of the original document, you wouldn't be
very impressed would you?

Because LocoScript creates a backup copy like this, before
allowing you to edit your document, there must be enough space
on the disk for it to be able to do so. In fact if you plan to
add more text to your document then LocoScript will need more
than the existing document's size to store the edited version
of the document. Of course LocoScript normally doesn't erase
the original version until the current version has been saved
safely on the disk.

After you have been using LocoScript for a while and the
space on your disks has begun to fill up you may come across
this little problem while editing or attempting to save a
document:

```
        Error in: Drive A
        Disc is full
     ⇥ ● Run disc manager ⇤
        Cancel operation
```

You might not see this particular last option (it depends
on which version of LocoScript you have). Another version
allows you to ignore the error and continue. If this option is
selected then another menu is displayed warning that ignoring
error messages can seriously damage your file. That menu
invites you to cancel the operation or ignore the error and
continue. But you wouldn't get that far, would you? NEVER
ignore error messages. Remember, LocoScript is trying hard to
help you, it doesn't want you to lose your document, so heed
its warnings! Now back to the problem.

DON'T PANIC! LocoScript is telling you that it has tried
to save the current version of your document and that it has
failed because there isn't enough space left on the disk.
Provided that you follow these instructions carefully you
should not lose your document. The worst that could happen is
that LocoScript would abandon the current version and revert

to the original document. But you don't want that to happen so
please proceed with caution!

When this error message is displayed you MUST select the
Run disc manager option, so press <ENTER>. Doing this will
cause LocoScript to leave the *Editing text* menu temporarily
and display the *Disk management* menu.

Note the message in the Control zone reminding you to
make some space for your document. You see LocoScript really
is trying to help! Note also that LocoScript has stored a part
of your document in a file ending in the filetype or extension
$$$.

You need to create some space (in this case on Drive A)
so move one of the largest documents from Drive A to Drive M
(don't forget to move it back before you switch off or reset
the PCW).

Don't try to move either the document that you were
editing or the $$$ file. Do NOT erase this file.

When you have made some space on the disk, press <EXIT>
and LocoScript will return to the *Editing text* menu and should
continue saving your document. Provided all goes well
LocoScript will save your document, delete the original and
delete the $$$ file.

You can avoid the whole problem by keeping an eye on the
remaining free space (via the *Disk management* menu); bear in
mind that you need twice as much space as initially seems
necessary.

If anything goes wrong during this process and LocoScript
cannot save the current version then you might end up with the
original document if you are very unlucky. While this is
unlikely to happen you should be prepared, it therefore makes
sense to regularly use the *Save and continue* option so that if
it does happen then all you have lost are the most recent
changes that you have made since you last saved the document.

3.1.3 – P=Print document (*Disk management* menu option)

This option is described in Chapter 4.

3.1.4 – D=Direct printing (*Disk management* menu option)

This option is also described in Chapter 4.

3.2 - BASIC WORD PROCESSING FACILITIES

You will need to practise using LocoScript; this is best done
with a document comprising several pages, as this is more than
can be displayed on the screen at one time. So choose a
relatively large one to work on. If you haven't already created
a suitable document of your own, then you might like to use one
Amstrad have supplied e.g. READ.ME.

Starting with the *Disk management* menu on the screen,
use:

> ⟨SHIFT⟩+⟨←⟩
> ⟨SHIFT⟩+⟨→⟩
> ⟨SHIFT⟩+⟨↑⟩
> ⟨SHIFT⟩+⟨↓⟩

to move the *group* cursor into the box called Drive A (you
might find that this cursor is already in this box). Then move
the *group* cursor over the group called LETTERS.

Notice that LocoScript automatically places the *file*
cursor in the A:LETTERS column, for you.

Next, use the ⟨↑⟩ or ⟨↓⟩ keys to position the *file* cursor
over the document called READ.ME, in the A:LETTERS column.

When the *file* cursor is over READ.ME, press ⟨E⟩.
E=Edit existing document. Pressing this key invokes a
pull-down menu like this:

> Edit document:
> ⇥ Name: READ   .ME ⇤
> Group: LETTERS
> Drive: A

Press ⟨ENTER⟩ to load the document called READ.ME into
the PCW's memory and display it on the screen. Now you can
experiment with the cursor and text positioning keys with
impunity. If you type in characters, the *character* cursor shows
you where the next character that you type will appear.

If you haven't used a word processor before then you will
need to 'play around' for a while in order to get a feel for
the way it works. Don't worry about spoiling the document, as
LocoScript will automatically keep a backup copy stored safely
on disk for you, just in case you decide to abandon what you
are doing. If you experiment and have some fun now, you will
gain confidence, so that when you come to do some more serious
work later, you will be less likely to get into difficulty.

Holding most keys down will cause the character (or function) to be repeated; this is called autorepeat.

If you move far enough down through the document, using the cursor and text positioning keys, you will see the disk drive light come on again; don't worry, the PCW will just be loading some more of the document into its memory.

When you have finished practising, you will be able to abandon the edited version of the document; if you do this LocoScript will revert automatically to the backup copy, which is held on disk, so you won't lose anything. Don't abandon just yet though, try out a few other operations first.

If you are a fast typist you may find the display a bit slow at times. However, you can always continue typing at your own speed, LocoScript will catch up with you eventually. Sometimes you will need to give LocoScript a series of instructions, just type them in and leave the machine to get on with it!

3.2.1 – Cursor control and text positioning keys

An important feature of any word processor is those facilities which are provided to help you move a cursor around within the text that you produce, and for moving that text around the screen. In addition to the normal cursor positioning keys, the PCW provides additional text positioning keys (Amstrad call these textual movement keys).

3.2.1.1 – Cursor control keys ⟨←⟩, ⟨→⟩, ⟨↑⟩ and ⟨↓⟩ when used with ⟨SHIFT⟩ and ⟨ALT⟩

You already know that pressing ⟨←⟩, ⟨→⟩, ⟨↑⟩ or ⟨↓⟩, moves the cursor:

             ⟨←⟩ left one character
             ⟨→⟩ right one character
             ⟨↑⟩ up one line
             ⟨↓⟩ down one line

You will find that pressing ⟨←⟩, ⟨→⟩, ⟨↑⟩ or ⟨↓⟩, while ⟨SHIFT⟩ is depressed, moves the cursor in larger steps. Note that you need to press ⟨SHIFT⟩ first, and then while it is held down, press ⟨←⟩, ⟨→⟩, ⟨↑⟩ or ⟨↓⟩.

```
<SHIFT>+<←> left 40 characters
<SHIFT>+<→> right 40 characters
<SHIFT>+<↑> up 20 lines
<SHIFT>+<↓> down 20 lines
```

If any of the above are preceded by ⟨ALT⟩, then the document will move and the cursor will stay still. Pressing ⟨ALT⟩ in conjunction with these keys, allows you to move the screen relative to the document.

Note that you need to press both ⟨ALT⟩ and ⟨SHIFT⟩ together, and then while they are both held down, press ⟨←⟩, ⟨→⟩, ⟨↑⟩ or ⟨↓⟩. The arrow indicates the direction in which you are moving the screen. For example, if ⟨ALT⟩+⟨SHIFT⟩+⟨↑⟩ are pressed, then you will see the document scroll down, while the screen apparently moves up.

3.2.1.2 – Text positioning keys ⟨LINE⟩/⟨EOL⟩, ⟨DOC⟩/⟨PAGE⟩, ⟨PARA⟩ and ⟨WORD⟩/⟨CHAR⟩ when used with ⟨ALT⟩

Pressing ⟨LINE⟩/⟨EOL⟩, ⟨DOC⟩/⟨PAGE⟩, ⟨PARA⟩ or ⟨WORD⟩/⟨CHAR⟩ also moves the cursor. If you precede these keys with ⟨ALT⟩, their action is reversed:

⟨EOL⟩ to the end of the current line, then to the end of the next line
⟨ALT⟩+⟨EOL⟩ to the end of the previous line

⟨LINE⟩ (i.e. ⟨SHIFT⟩+⟨EOL⟩) to the beginning of the next line
⟨ALT⟩+⟨LINE⟩ to the beginning of the previous line

⟨PAGE⟩ to the beginning of the next page
⟨ALT⟩+⟨PAGE⟩ to the beginning of the previous page

⟨DOC⟩ (i.e. ⟨SHIFT⟩+⟨PAGE⟩) to the end of the document
⟨ALT⟩+⟨DOC⟩ to the beginning of the document

⟨PARA⟩ to the beginning of the next paragraph
⟨ALT⟩+⟨PARA⟩ to the beginning of the previous paragraph

```
<CHAR> to the next character
<ALT>+<CHAR> to the previous character

<WORD> (i.e. <SHIFT>+<CHAR>) to the next word
<ALT>+<WORD> to the previous word
```

Note that <LINE>, <DOC> and <WORD> are obtained using <SHIFT>. If you want to move forward two pages in your document simply press <PAGE> twice; if you want to move back two pages press <ALT>+<PAGE>, twice.

The <STOP> key can be used to stop some actions. For example if you press <DOC> (i.e. <SHIFT>+<PAGE>) to move the cursor to the end of the document and then press <STOP> the cursor will stop temporarily. The message *STOP: Press STOP again to STOP, ENTER to continue or any other character*, will be displayed in the bottom line of the Control zone.

If you no longer want the cursor to move to the end of the document press <STOP> again, otherwise press any other key. Note that you cannot use <STOP> when saving a document; LocoScript will ignore the command and finish saving your document.

When you feel you have had enough practice, press <EXIT>, which invokes a pull-down menu. To abandon the edited version, press <↓> three times, so that the pull-down menu looks like this (otherwise press <CAN> to continue editing):

```
        Exit options:
        Finish editing
        Save and Continue
        Save and Print
     ⇥ ● Abandon edit        ⇤
```

Now press <ENTER> and allow a few seconds for the display to return to the *Disk management* menu.

3.2.2 - The <UNIT> key and *UniT* code

When you read about <PARA> in the previous section, you probably wondered about the purpose of <UNIT>, (i.e. <SHIFT>+<PARA>). You can place codes or markers, called *UniTs*, in your text and then use <UNIT> to return to them later. So <UNIT> is used to locate *UniT* markers. To try out <UNIT> you need a long document. So once again, from the *Disk management* menu, reload the document called READ.ME, back into the PCW's memory, as you did earlier.

Move the *group* cursor over the LETTERS group, and then move the *file* cursor over the document called READ.ME and press <E>, followed by <ENTER>.

Before you go any further, you need to ensure that all the special word processing embedded commands in the document, will be shown on the screen. Embedded commands, or codes, are special instructions which tell LocoScript how to format the text. You can choose to have all these codes displayed, or not, as you wish. The codes themselves are not printed; their purpose is to control how your text is printed.

In the third line of the Control zone, at the top of the screen, you will see *f1=Show*. Press <f1> to invoke the pull-down menu, and then press <[+]> (i.e. the *Set* key). Pressing <[+]> makes a tick appear alongside *Codes*.

Now press <ENTER> and look at the screen closely. You should be able to see some codes embedded in the document. These codes are always enclosed in parentheses and many are preceded by + or -, for example (+UL) or (Centre). Don't worry about what these codes do, at this stage; this is explained more fully in Chapter 3.3 and Chapter 3.4. The *Show* menu itself is explained more fully in Chapter 3.3.6.1.

You can think of a *UniT* as being a subdivision, or section, of your document which you can choose to make any size. For example, if you are using LocoScript to prepare a report, then you might choose to divide your report into a number of units. You would then mark the beginning of each unit, in the document, with the (UniT) code.

To try this, move the cursor down a few lines and then press <[+]> immediately followed by <U> and <T> (U and T can be UPPER or lower case). You should see the code (UniT), appear in the document, where you previously left the flashing cursor. Codes like this can be deleted using <DEL→> or <←DEL>.

If after pressing <[+]>, you are slow in pressing the <U> and <T>, then you will see a long pull-down menu appear. This is called the *Set* menu (see Chapter 3.5.1). Instead of waiting several seconds for the *Set* menu to appear, you can press the <[≡]> key, immediately after pressing <[+]>. Note that <[≡]> represents the key located between <←> and <→>. Also, notice that the U and T, of the UniT option, in the menu, are capital letters

Pressing <[+]>, quickly followed by <[≡]>, causes the *Set* menu to appear immediately. If you want to try this effect, then remember that you may cancel an unwanted menu at any time by pressing <CAN>.

With the *Set* menu displayed on the screen, use <↓> to move the *menu* cursor down to the *UniT* option, and then press <ENTER>. You will find that the *Set* menu disappears from the screen, and the (UniT) code appears in the document where you left the *character* cursor. This is how you mark the beginning of a unit. <UNIT> may be used to locate one of these codes. To locate this one, you will obviously need to start from somewhere else in the document.

So, to try out <UNIT>, move the *character* cursor back to the top of the document by pressing <ALT>+<DOC> (i.e. <ALT>+<SHIFT>+<PAGE>). When the cursor is back at the top of the document press <UNIT> (i.e. <SHIFT>+<PARA>), and the cursor will automatically move to the beginning of the unit.

Alternatively, move to the end of the document by pressing <DOC> (i.e. <SHIFT>+<PAGE>) and then press <ALT>+<UNIT> (i.e. <ALT>+<SHIFT>+<PARA>) to move the cursor back to the beginning of the unit.

So, to recap, you can either:

press <[+]>, immediately followed by <U> and then <T> (this inserts the (UniT) code in the document directly)

or press <[+]>, quickly followed by <[≡]>, to prompt the *Set* menu (and then select the *UniT* option as described above)

or press <[+]>, and wait a few seconds for the *Set* menu to appear (and then select the *UniT* option as described above).

<UNIT> can be handy when using the *Save and Continue* option of the *Edit options* menu; this is described in Chapter 3.1.1.2. *UniT* markers are saved with your document so if you place one in your document before selecting the *Finish editing* option of the *Edit options* menu, then you will be able to use it a bit like a book marker, to find your place later.

3.2.3 - Document editing functions

Once again, you will need to have a suitable document in the PCW's memory, so that you can experiment. To learn to use the

word processor successfully, you need to practise using its
different features as much as possible. Don't worry about
spoiling your working copy disk, just make sure that you don't
use your master disks.

Word processors are popular because they make the task
of editing text so easy. Generally, when you edit an existing
document you want either to insert more text, to delete some of
the existing text, to copy some of the text from one place to
another or just to move some text from one place to another.
Being able to search for and replace strings of characters in
the document is important too.

When editing text, it helps to be able to see any
embedded word processing codes which already exist in your
document. LocoScript enables you either to show or. to hide
these codes. To make sure that they will be shown on the
screen press <f1>, to invoke the *Show* menu. Ensure that there
is a tick against *Codes* in this menu. Use <↓> and <↑> to
position the *menu* cursor then press <[+]> followed by <ENTER>.

3.2.3.1 – Inserting text and using the <RELAY> key

You have already seen in Chapter 3.1.2 that LocoScript allows
you to add more text to a document, quite freely. Before adding
more text you should make sure that all codes will be
displayed, otherwise you might end up with codes added where
they are not wanted. Use the *Show* menu to check this.

The only other problem is that as you insert more text,
the layout will become messy, so you will need to relay the
paragraph that you are working on. If you find this quirk of
LocoScript's disconcerting, you can always relay the paragraph
by pressing <RELAY>, at any time. If you don't use this key,
you will find that LocoScript relays the paragraph for you
automatically when you move the cursor down to the next
paragraph, or before the document is saved on disk.

While most other word processors relay your text
automatically for you, as you work, they tend to be more
expensive. Word processors generally enable you to choose
between inserting your new text in between the existing text
or overwriting the existing text with your new text.
Unfortunately, LocoScript doesn't give you a choice; it always
inserts new text, hence you may need to delete some of the
existing text.

3.2.3.2 – Deleting text using the <CUT> key

Before deleting text you should make sure that all codes will
be displayed, otherwise an unwanted code might be left behind
in your text. Use the *Show* menu to check this.

To delete a block of text, position the cursor on the
first character of the block to be deleted, and press <CUT>.
Look at the third line of the Control zone, at the top of your
screen, and you will see *CUT: select area then press CUT to
remove permanently, CANCEL to abandon.* Now position the cursor
one character to the right of the last character in the block
that you want to delete.

The area covered is highlighted and if you move the
cursor back, this area is reduced. When you have decided on the
extent of the text to be cut from the document, press <CUT>
again. The highlighted area will disappear from the screen and
with it the block that you want to delete.

If after pressing <CUT> for the first time you change
your mind, then pressing <CAN> will cancel the command. After
using <CUT>, you will probably need to relay the text. You can
do this either by pressing <RELAY>, or by moving the cursor to
the next paragraph.

3.2.3.3 – Copying text using the <COPY> key

Before adding more text, make sure that all codes will be
displayed, otherwise an unwanted code might be added to your
text. Use the *Show* menu to check this.

To duplicate a block of text in your document, position
the cursor on the first character of the block to be copied,
and press <COPY>. Look at the third line of the Control zone,
at the top of your screen, and you will see *CUT: select area
then press CUT to save & remove, COPY to save, CANCEL to
abandon.* Now position the cursor one character to the right of
the last character in the block that you want to copy.

The area covered is highlighted and if you move the
cursor back up, the highlighted area is reduced. When you have
decided on the extent of the text to be copied, press <COPY>
again, followed by any number between 0 and 9. The highlighted
area will disappear from the screen leaving your original text
intact.

Note that LocoScript allows you store up to 10 different
blocks for copying; this is explained more fully in
Chapter 3.2.4.1.

Now move the cursor to the point in your text where you
want the copy to be inserted, and press <PASTE>, followed by
the number you selected.

If after pressing <COPY> for the first time, you change
your mind, then pressing <CAN> will cancel the command. After
using <COPY>, you will probably need to relay the text, you
can do this by pressing <RELAY>, or by moving the cursor to
the next paragraph.

During the preparation of this book and while attempting
to move a block from the end of a large (43K) document to the
top, LocoScript version 1.2 displayed the following:

```
        Error in: Editor
        Unexpected end of file
        Cancel operation
     ⅃ ● Ignore error and continue ⌐
```

Not wanting to lose the current version the decision made
was to ignore the error and continue; LocoScript displayed
another warning!

```
        Error in: Editor
        WARNING: Ignoring errors can
        seriously damage your file
     ⅃ ● Cancel operation            ⌐
```

Obviously a warning like that cannot be ignored. All the
amendments made to the document since it had previously been
saved were lost; LocoScript reverted to the backup copy of the
document, so it wasn't a total disaster. The moral of this
story is to keep documents small and then merge them into one
large document prior to printing and also use the *Save and
continue* option regularly. While this has been mentioned
several times already its importance cannot be over
emphasised.

In the unlikely event of this happening to you please
report it to Amstrad. Ideally send them your document or file
on a disk together with a covering letter.

3.2.3.4 - Moving text using the <COPY>, <CUT> and <PASTE> keys

Before moving text, make sure that all codes will be displayed, otherwise an unwanted one might be added to your text. Use the *Show menu* to check this.

To move a block of text in your document from one place to another, position the cursor on the first character of the text to be moved and press <COPY>. Look at the third line of the Control zone, at the top of your screen, and you will see *CUT: select area then press CUT to save & remove, COPY to save, CANCEL to abandon.* Now position the cursor one character to the right of the last character in the block that you want to copy.

Once again the area covered is highlighted and if you move the cursor back up, the highlighted area is reduced. When you have decided on the extent of the text to be moved, press <CUT>, followed by any number between 0 and 9. The highlighted area will disappear from the screen and with it the text that you have chosen to relocate.

Now move the cursor to the point in your text where you want the copy to be added, and press <PASTE>, followed by the number you selected.

3.2.3.5 - Searching for text using the <FIND> key

<FIND> can be used to locate a string of characters, of up to 30 in length. LocoScript will begin its search starting from the position that you left the cursor in, and will move forward through your document. If you want to search all of your document for the string then you must first move the cursor to the top of first page, by pressing <ALT>+<DOC> (i.e. <ALT>+<SHIFT>+<PAGE>).

Press <FIND>, and type in your string, including the carriage return if required, then press <ENTER>. The cursor will stop at the first occurrence of the string. Pressing <FIND> followed by <ENTER> will prompt LocoScript to move forward to the next occurrence, and so on. If LocoScript cannot find the string it will move the cursor to the end of the document.

When deleting blocks of text, <FIND> can be used to locate the last character of the section to be deleted. Move the cursor to the beginning of the text to be deleted, press <CUT>, then press <FIND> and type the string (e.g. the last word, together with its full stop (or period)) and press <ENTER>. A highlighted section will extend to the character found; when you are sure that it is correct, press <CUT> again to delete the block of text.

3.2.3.6 – Replacing text using the ⟨EXCH⟩ key

⟨EXCH⟩ is used to swap one string of characters for another. Once again the maximum length is 30 characters. Pressing ⟨EXCH⟩ (i.e. ⟨SHIFT⟩+⟨FIND⟩) invokes a pull-down menu like this:

```
      Exchange_____
    ⇥ Find:                            ⇤
      Exch:_____
    ● Confirm each exchange
      Automatic exchange to end of PARA
      Automatic exchange to end of PAGE
      Automatic exchange to end of DOC
```

First, type in the *Find* string. Next, press ⟨↓⟩, and enter the *Exch* string, followed by ⟨ENTER⟩.

If you look at page 71, of Amstrad's User Guide, you will find it suggests that you press ⟨ENTER⟩, instead of ⟨↓⟩. If you do this, the pull-down menu will disappear from the screen and the cursor will move to the first occurrence of the *Find* string. You cannot use ⟨PARA⟩, ⟨PAGE⟩ or ⟨DOC⟩ as they suggest; if you try, the PCW will just beep at you. It would be safer to press ⟨CAN⟩, to abandon. If you press ⟨ENTER⟩, but leave the *Exch* string blank, the string that is found will be replaced with blank!

Now look at the third line of the Control zone where you will see displayed *EXCH: Press [+] to exchange and continue, [-] to simply continue, or CANCEL to abandon.*

If you follow these instructions you shouldn't have any difficulty. So, after typing the *Find* string, followed by pressing ⟨↓⟩, then typing the second string and finally pressing ⟨ENTER⟩, LocoScript will move the cursor to the first occurrence of the *Find* string. If you press ⟨[+]⟩ the *Find* string will be replaced by the *Exch* string. If, instead, you press ⟨[-]⟩, then LocoScript will move the cursor to the next occurrence of the *Find* string.

You can abandon the exchange process at any time by pressing ⟨CAN⟩. Of course, if LocoScript can't locate the *Find* string at all, then the cursor will be moved to the end of the document. LocoScript will commence its search for the *Find* string starting where you left the cursor, so if you want to exchange every occurrence of a word in a document, then you must use ⟨ALT⟩+⟨DOC⟩ (i.e. ⟨ALT⟩+⟨SHIFT⟩+⟨PAGE⟩) to move the cursor to the beginning of your document, before you press ⟨EXCH⟩.

Notice that the option you get by default, in the pull-down menu, is *Confirm each exchange*, which means that the exchange will not occur until you press <[+]>. You can select one of the other options, by using <↓> to move the tick down to the option you want, before pressing <ENTER>.

If you have used a word processor before you might have got into the habit of using the exchange facility to save you the effort of typing the same phrases repeatedly. For example, if you were writing a paper about eels and their migratory habits you would probably need to type the words 'Sargasso Sea' quite a few times. Instead of typing 'Sargasso Sea' you could just type 'sar' and then use the exchange facility later to turn every occurrence of 'sar' into 'Sargasso Sea'. However, LocoScript provides an even more elegant solution to this particular problem; see Chapter 3.2.4.2!

3.2.4 - Blocks (0 to 9) and Phrases (A to Z)

LocoScript allows you to label sections of text in your document and then store them, so that later they can either be reinserted elsewhere in the same document, or be moved to a different document. You are provided with two different methods for labelling sections of text within your document. The *Blocks* method enables you to save large sections of text up to a whole document, whereas the *Phrases* method is intended for small groups of words. Note that Blocks and Phrases are stored as non-document files.

3.2.4.1 - Using blocks with the <COPY>, <CUT> and <PASTE> keys

In Chapter 3.2.3.3 you followed <COPY> with a number between 0 and 9, similarly in Chapter 3.2.3.4 you followed <CUT> with a number between 0 and 9. Supposing you used 0 in both cases, what you actually did was to instruct LocoScript to store your text in block 0 for you. When you pressed <PASTE>, LocoScript reinserted the block into your document. LocoScript provides 10 such blocks for storing text, numbered 0 to 9. The text remains in the block until you replace it with something else, or until you finish editing the document. You can use <PASTE> to insert the same block more than once, because the original copy remains intact.

If you look at the Control zone, you will see f8=Blocks.
Press <f8> (i.e. <SHIFT>+<f7>) to invoke this pull-down menu:

    Text storage:
    Block
  ⇥ Save block   ? ⇤
    Phrase

    Save all phrases

Notice that although this menu is divided into two
sections (i.e. Block and Phrase), we are only concerned with
the first at this stage. The *Block* section shows you which
blocks, if any, currently have text stored in them. If you
used block 0, then the pull-down menu would look like this:

    Text storage:
    Block   0
  ⇥ Save block   ? ⇤
    Phrase

    Save all phrases

Note that the contents of all blocks are lost when you
finish editing your document, unless you save them on disk
before you press <EXIT>. To save a block on disk, use the *Save
block* option of the *Blocks menu*, then type the number of the
block, followed by <ENTER>. When you do this, LocoScript
changes from *the Editing text* menu to the *Disk management*
menu.

Look at the middle line of the Control zone and you will
see the following message displayed, *Pick destination Group and
Drive using cursor keys, then press ENTER, or CANCEL to
abandon*. If you follow these instructions and save your blocks
on your disk, LocoScript will return you to your document.

While blocks can be saved on disk, like documents, they
cannot be be edited in the same way; they are non-document
files. To display and make changes to a saved block, it must
first be inserted in an existing document.

Blocks or even whole documents, which have previously
been saved on disk, can be repeatedly inserted in or merged
with a document which is being edited. To do this invoke the
Modes menu using <f7>, while you are in the *Editing text* menu,
and use <↓> to select the *Insert text* option. When the menu

looks like this, press <ENTER>:

> Editor sub-modes :
> Edit Header
> Edit Identify text
> ⇥ ● Insert text   ⇤
> Disk management

When you press <ENTER>, LocoScript changes the display from the *Editing text* menu to the *Disk management* menu. If you look at the third line of the Control zone you will see displayed: *Use cursor keys to pick the file to insert, then press ENTER, or CANCEL to abandon.* When you press <ENTER> LocoScript returns the display to the *Editing text* menu and inserts the block or file, starting from where you left the cursor.

You can use the same procedure to insert previously saved ASCII text files, in your document. ASCII is an abbreviation for the American Standard Code for Information Interchange, which was introduced in 1963, and is the system used to give code numbers to each of the keyboard characters. Before a computer can store text, each character must first be converted into its ASCII code, as computers can only store and manipulate numbers. ASCII text files that have been prepared using CP/M may be used with LocoScript. See Chapter 2.7.1.7 for more information.

3.2.4.2 – Using phrases with the <COPY>, <CUT> and <PASTE> keys

LocoScript allows a maximum of 26 short phrases to be stored, labelled A to Z, which can be pasted anywhere in a document. While individual phrases can be a maximum of 255 characters long, their total length is limited to 550 characters, hence you cannot always use all 26 phrases.

The master disk that Amstrad supplies with the PCW, has a file on it called PHRASES.STD which includes some example phrases. If your working copy of this disk includes this file, then you can try this facility while editing a document, by pressing <PASTE> followed by Z. The *Blocks menu* shows you which phrases currently hold text.

Phrases that have been saved on disk, are stored in a special file called PHRASES.STD, this file MUST be in group 0 of Drive A. PHRASES.STD is loaded into the PCW's memory, whenever LocoScript is loaded and hence its phrases are always available for use.

To save a phrase of your own, move the cursor to its first character and press <COPY>, and then move the cursor to the end of the phrase. If you want to leave the phrase in your document, press <COPY> again, followed by a letter. Otherwise, if you want to erase it, press <CUT>, followed by a letter. If the letter you select is already in use, then the original phrase will be replaced, temporarily, by your new one. You will now be able to invoke your phrase, simply by pressing <PASTE>, followed by the letter.

Notice, that when you finish editing, your new phrase will be lost, unless you save it first. You can save it by using the *Blocks* menu. Select the *Save all phrases* option and then press <ENTER>. Doing this automatically creates a file called PHRASES.STD in group 0 of Drive M, saves all existing phrases in this file, and returns you to the *Editing text* menu.

To save new phrases more permanently, on disk, you must move the PHRASES.STD file from Drive M, to group 0 on Drive A. If a PHRASES.STD file already exists in this group, then you will have either to delete it, or rename it, before copying the PHRASES.STD file.

You can copy files while still in the *Editing text* menu by selecting the *Disk management* option of the *Modes* menu.

When you have selected this option press <ENTER> and LocoScript will change the display to the *Disk management* menu. When you have copied the file, press <EXIT>, to return to the *Editing text* menu.

If you don't move the PHRASES.STD file from Drive M to Drive A, then the PHRASES.STD file in Drive M will be lost when you switch the PCW off, and the original PHRASES.STD file will be used next time you load in LocoScript.

You can use phrases to store lines of text which have lots of control codes in them thus saving a lot of time and effort.

Note that to delete a code you need either to place the cursor on the left-hand parenthesis (i.e. '(') and press <DEL→> or place the cursor on the right-hand parenthesis (i.e. ')') and press <←>.

3.2.5 – Special key combinations

<ALT>+<ENTER>   acts   as   a   caps   lock   key   alternately

setting/clearing characters (except Greek) in UPPER case. Note the *Caps* indicator in the top right-hand corner of the Control zone.

<ALT>+<RELAY> alternately sets/clears the numeric keypad (the keys to the right of the function keys). Note the *Num* indicator in the top right-hand corner of the Control zone.

Note that if you have both *Caps* and *Num* on, LocoScript displays *C+N* in the Control zone. Also note that you cannot exit from the *Editing text* menu while *Num* or *C+N* are on.

<SHIFT>+<EXTRA>+<EXIT> resets the computer to the state it was in when LocoScript was loaded; the contents of the memory are destroyed.

3.3 — CHANGING THE LAYOUT OF YOUR DOCUMENT
(Both global and local changes)

Apart from making alterations to the text itself, word processors enable you to make fundamental changes to the way the text, as a whole, is arranged or laid out. This is referred to as the format or layout of your document. LocoScript provides you with a number of different methods for controlling the layout of your documents, but the most important of these is the use of standard templates.

A standard template is like a document, insofar as it can be stored on disk and can be edited. The difference is that standard templates are used to control the way your text is formatted. This means that when you create a document, its basic layout is determined by a standard template.

A change which affects the whole layout of the document is a global change. To do this you have to edit the *Base layout*. You can also make changes to the layout of your text within your document if you want to; these local changes do not affect the Base layout.

As you know, the disk drives are divided into 8 groups. Each group is intended to have a standard template associated with it. The standard template document for each group must be named TEMPLATE.STD. Whenever you create a new document, LocoScript uses that group's TEMPLATE.STD document as the basis for its layout. Therefore, you should get into the habit of categorising your documents by group.

You need to make sure that each group has a suitable standard template. For example, you might want a group called LETTERS; this must have a TEMPLATE.STD document for letters. A group called MEMOS must have a TEMPLATE.STD document for memos, etc. Note that these two TEMPLATE.STD documents would be quite different. You would then put all your letters in the LETTERS group, and put all your memos in the MEMOS group.

If you attempt to create a new document from a group which doesn't have a TEMPLATE.STD file, then LocoScript will create a TEMPLATE.STD document for you, automatically; but this is unlikely to be exactly what you want. To avoid this happening, and to ensure that you get exactly the layout that you want, you are advised to create suitable TEMPLATE.STD documents for each of the groups that you are going to use.

3.3.1 – Creating a standard group template i.e TEMPLATE.STD

Suppose you needed to set up a TEMPLATE.STD document for a group that didn't already have one. You could create it by selecting *C=Create document* from the *Disk management* menu.

LocoScript would try to help you, by checking to see if there is a document called TEMPLATE.STD, in group 7, on Drive M. If it could not find one there, it would try to use one from group 0, Drive A. If it still couldn't find one, then it would try to use one from group 0, Drive M. If all else failed, it would create a template which is suitable for A4 paper, and provide a character pitch of 12 characters per inch, which is standard.

If this sounds like quite a rigmarole, then you'll be pleased to hear that Amstrad have provided about 15 sample templates, some of which might suit your requirements. If you look at the *Disk management* menu, you will see a group called TEMPLATE. This group contains some of the sample templates; the LETTERS and CONT groups already have TEMPLATE.STD documents.

To be able to use one of the examples, you will need to copy it from the TEMPLATE group to your new group, making sure that you rename the file, so that it becomes TEMPLATE.STD. Then, whenever you create a document in your new group, LocoScript will automatically use that TEMPLATE.STD file, instead of one from another group.

In order to be able to experiment, you need to create a TEMPLATE.STD document in a group that is empty. If group 7 on

your working disk in Drive A has not been used, then this will
be ideal. First you need to rename the group from group 7 to
something else e.g. TEST. If you look at the *Disk management*
menu you will see an option called f5=Rename; now position the
group cursor over Drive A: group 7 and then press <f5>. Doing
this will invoke a pull-down menu. Press <↓> twice to move the
tick down to the *rename Group* option, like this:

```
    rename document
    recover from Limbo
 ⇥ ● rename Group        ⇤
    rename Disk
```

Press <ENTER> and another pull-down menu like this will
appear.

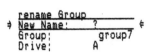
```
    rename Group
 ⇥ New Name:    ?      ⇤
    Group:         group7
    Drive:       A
```

Type TEST and then press <ENTER>. Now you are ready to
create a TEMPLATE.STD document for this group. If you look at
the *Disk management* menu you will see the option C=Create new
document. When the *group* cursor is over Drive A: TEST, press
<C> to invoke another pull-down menu like this:

```
    Create document
 ⇥ Name:  DOCUMENT.000 ⇤
    Group:  TEST
    Drive:  A
```

Now carefully type TEMPLATESTD, and when you have done
that, press <ENTER>. You will see that LocoScript automatically
inserts a full stop (or period) between TEMPLATE and STD. Note
also that LocoScript allows you to type filenames in either
UPPER or lower case letters, but it always displays them in
UPPER case letters.

The cursor will be at the top of an apparently empty
document. At the left-hand end of the Control zone, you will
see :-:Layout. This tells you that the Base layout
(i.e. :-:Layout) is being used. The Base layout is the global
layout that applies to the document as a whole. It is possible
to have local layouts in your documents, but it is always the
Base layout that you start with, when you create a document.

What you are doing is setting up the TEMPLATE.STD
document for the last group on Drive A, which is now called
TEST. In future, when you create documents in this group, it
will be this TEMPLATE.STD document which will determine their
Base layouts.

So, to rename a group:

        position the *group* cursor over the group
        press ⟨f5⟩ to invoke the *Rename* menu
        press ⟨↓⟩ twice to select the *rename Group* option
        press ⟨ENTER⟩ to invoke the *rename Group* menu
        type the new group name
        press ⟨ENTER⟩

To create a standard template:

        press ⟨C⟩ to create a new document
        type TEMPLATESTD
        press ⟨ENTER⟩

It is important to realise that standard templates are just like ordinary documents. The only difference is that, when you create a new document, it inherits its Base layout from the group's TEMPLATE.STD document. Standard template documents can be created, edited, copied, moved, and erased just like other documents. As TEMPLATE.STD's are documents they can be printed; you might find it useful to make hardcopy printouts of your TEMPLATE.STD's for reference.

3.3.2 – *Editing base layout* menu (3rd line of Control zone)
(Making global changes to the layout)

You have probably noticed that there is a line with numbers on it just below the Control zone; this is called the *ruler line*. The ruler line controls the layout of the page body in your document. The ruler line normally has 3 parts to it: the left margin, the page body and the right margin. The solid lines, at the left and right-hand ends, govern the width of the margins; the width of the page body is governed by the length of the dotted line; the shorter the dotted line the narrower your text will be.

For example, you might want a document that is going to be printed on A4 paper to have 1-inch margins, left and right. Imagine that, in addition, you need to position a photograph half-way down on the left-hand side; obviously you will need to be able to indent the left-hand margin by at least the width of the photograph. LocoScript enables you to do this, by allowing you to have more than one layout in the same document. Your document would use the Base layout at the top and bottom, but a different layout would be required for the section in the middle, to the right of the photograph.

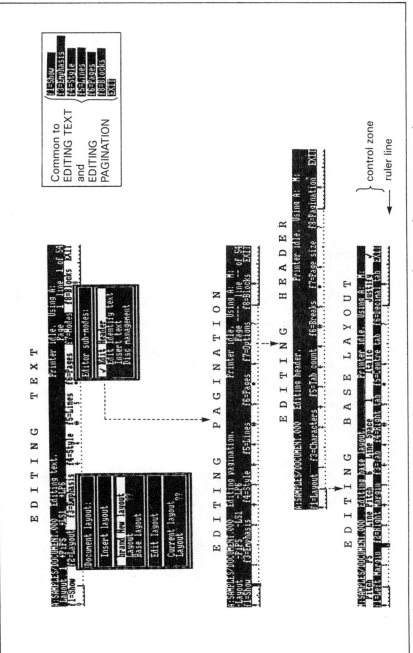

Accessing 'EDITING BASE LAYOUT' from 'EDITING TEXT'

In order to set up the Base layout, you will need to invoke LocoScript's *Editing base layout* menu. Look at the Control zone and you will see the menu option f7=Modes; press <f7> to invoke a pull-down menu like this:

```
        Editor sub-menus:
     ⇥ ● Edit Header            ⇤
        Edit Identify text
        Insert text
        Disk management
```

Press <ENTER> to select the *Edit Header* option; the display will change and show LocoScript's *Editing pagination* menu. Select f7=Options; press <f7> to invoke the *Editing header* menu. Select the f1=Layout option; press <f1> to invoke the *Editing base layout* menu.

So, to invoke the *Editing base layout* menu from the *Editing text* menu:

> press <f7> to invoke the *Editor sub-menus* menu
> press <ENTER> to select the *Edit Header* option
> press <f7> to select *f7=Options*
> press <f1> to select *f1=Layout*

3.3.2.1 – f1=Left Margin (*Editing base layout* menu option)

To alter the margins in the ruler line (in the *Editing base layout* menu), press <↓>. When you do this you will see the *menu* cursor in the middle line of the Control zone disappear and at the same time a *ruler line* cursor will appear in the ruler line. Note that you can return to the *menu* cursor by pressing <↑>.

Now, by using <→> and <←>, position the *ruler line* cursor over the number 1 in the ruler line and then press <f1>, to obtain a left-hand margin of approximately 1 inch. Notice how the solid line, which represents the left-hand margin, extends from the left-hand side of the screen to the number 1 in the ruler line.

3.3.2.2 – f2=Right Margin (*Editing base layout* menu option)

Now move the *ruler line* cursor so that it covers the number 7 in the ruler line and press <f2> (i.e. <SHIFT>+<f1>), to position the right-hand margin 6 inches from the left-hand margin. The right-hand margin should now extend from the right-hand side of the screen to the number 7 in the ruler line.

So, to change the left and right-hand margin settings of

the base layout:

> press ⟨↓⟩ to invoke the *ruler line* cursor
> press ⟨→⟩ or ⟨←⟩ to position the *ruler line* cursor
> press ⟨f1⟩ to set the left-hand margin
> press ⟨→⟩ or ⟨←⟩ to position the *ruler line* cursor
> press ⟨f2⟩ to set the left-hand margin

When you have done this, you will need to save your new TEMPLATE.STD document. In the bottom right-hand corner of the Control zone you will see the option EXIT. Press ⟨EXIT⟩ and notice that LocoScript changes from its *Editing base layout* menu to its *Editing header* menu, where you will see another EXIT option. So, press ⟨EXIT⟩ again, and a pull-down menu like this will appear.

```
    Finish altering options
→ ● Confirm                    ←
    Cancel
```

Press ⟨ENTER⟩ to select *Confirm*, and LocoScript will change to its *Editing pagination* menu, where once again you will find another EXIT option. Press ⟨EXIT⟩ to invoke yet another pull-down menu, like this:

```
    Exit pagination editing:
→ ● Use this pagination ←
    Recover old pagination
    Empty pagination text
    Abandon edit altogether
```

Press ⟨ENTER⟩ to select *Use this pagination* and LocoScript will return to its *Editing text* menu. Finally press ⟨EXIT⟩ once more, followed by ⟨ENTER⟩ in order to return to the *Disk management* menu.

So, to return to the *Disk management* menu from the *Editing base layout* menu:

> press ⟨EXIT⟩ to return to the *Editing header* menu
> press ⟨EXIT⟩ to *Finish altering options*
> press ⟨ENTER⟩ to return to *Editing pagination* menu
> press ⟨EXIT⟩ to *Exit pagination editing*
> press ⟨ENTER⟩ to return to *Editing text* menu
> press ⟨EXIT⟩ to return to *Finish editing*
> press ⟨ENTER⟩ to return to *Disk management* menu

What you have done is created a TEMPLATE.STD document, in the group called TEST, on drive A. You have set up a Base layout with the left-hand margin set to 1 and the right-hand margin set to 7. While this may seem to be a lengthy and complex process, you will find that with a little practice you can press the keys in a matter of seconds (LocoScript may take a little longer to catch up with you, though).

Bearing in mind that A4 paper is approximately 8 inches wide, you might expect that, having set the left and right-hand margins to 1 and 7, respectively, this would produce the 1-inch margins wanted. Well, not quite! By now you are probably beginning to think that setting margin stops on a typewriter must be easier! This may well be true, but a typewriter can't do everything that a word processor can, and anyway once you have set up the margins in a standard template you don't have to worry about them again.

If you look at the bail bar on the printer, you will see what are apparently 1-inch graduations. While the bail bar is graduated in steps of 1-inch and this appears to correspond with the ruler line graduations which are displayed on the screen, it is not that simple.

Just consider some of the things that are going to affect the final width of the margins. If you ignore the effect that the ruler line has for the moment, you still have to consider the lateral position of the paper in the printer and the width of the paper itself. For the purpose of this discussion it is assumed that you are going to use A4 paper, and that the left-hand edge will always be positioned in line with the 1, which is engraved on the bail bar. It is always a good idea to be consistent about how you position the paper, whatever the width.

It is possible to vary the pitch of the characters and to have double-width characters (for details see Chapter 3.3.3.1). If you set the left-hand margin to 1.4 and the right-hand margin to 8.6 with Pitch=PS, then with the left-hand edge of your A4 paper in line with the 1 on the bail bar, this will result in the 1-inch margins that you wanted. If you want to make this change you will need to get back to the *Editing base layout* menu again; refer to Chapter 3.3.2 if you can't remember how to do this.

There seems to be a constant of 0.4" built into the left-hand margin.

If you want to change the left-hand margin from 1 to 1.4 and the right-hand margin from 7 to 8.6, you might also want to set Pitch=PS, Line Pitch=6, Line Space=1, Italic off and Justify on. This is explained in Chapter 3.3.3; you might prefer to wait until this section is reached and then make all of these changes at the same time.

When you have returned to the *Disk management* menu, with the *group* cursor positioned over the new group called TEST, press <C> to create a new document. A pull-down menu like this will appear:

<u>Create document</u>
→ Name: DOCUMENT.000 ←
   Group: TEST
   Drive: A

Notice, LocoScript suggests that you use the filename DOCUMENT.000. You can accept this, by pressing <ENTER>, if you like, or type in a name of your own choice. If you type in a name, e.g. TEST, notice that doing so overwrites the existing name DOCUMENT.000. In order to avoid the name TESTMENT.000 make sure that you press the space bar twice after typing TEST. When you are happy with the choice of filename, press <ENTER>.

LocoScript will open a new document which is based on the TEMPLATE.STD document that you created. Notice that the left and right margins are exactly as you set them up in the TEMPLATE.STD document. Any document created in the TEST group will automatically have the same margin settings. You can always edit the ruler line settings of the documents that you create if you want to; doing so will not affect the TEMPLATE.STD document or documents created subsequently, in the TEST group.

3.3.2.3 - f3=Tab (→) (*Editing base layout* menu option)

Generally speaking a tab is a point which is set in from the main left-hand margin by a specified amount that shows where lines can be started from on the screen. The term is derived from the tab stops which can be set on a typewriter. Tabs are used to produce columns, for starting paragraphs and so on.

LocoScript provides five different tabs:

(1) the (left) Tab →; this is the normal tab which is used to indent the first line of a paragraph from the left-hand margin

(2) the Indent Tab ↦; this is similar to the (left) Tab but the whole paragraph is indented instead of just the first line

(3) the Right Tab ←; this is used to line up the right-hand edge of a column

(4) the Centre Tab ↔; this is used to centre text around a particular point on the screen.

(5) the Decimal Tab *; this is used to line up decimal points in columns of numbers

Tab settings (with the exception of the Indent Tab) that have been created via the *Editing base layout* menu are displayed in the ruler line.

Assuming that tab settings exist in the ruler line (while creating a new document, editing an existing document or direct printing) if the *character* cursor is at the left-hand margin pressing <TAB> will move the *character* cursor to the first tab setting; pressing <TAB> again will move it to the next tab setting, and so on. Where the tab setting might be a (left) Tab, a Right Tab, a Centre Tab or a Decimal Tab.

Whenever you press <TAB> the tab character → will be inserted in your text. If you want to be able to see these tab characters in your document then you will have to place a tick alongside the *Effectors* option in the *Show* menu. Refer back to Chapter 3.2.2 if you don't know how to do this. Tab characters which have been placed in your document by pressing <TAB> can be deleted using <DEL→> or <←DEL>.

To set up (left) Tabs you need to invoke the *Editing base layout* menu. If you cannot remember how to do this refer back to Chapter 3.3.2. Press <↓> to invoke the *ruler line* cursor. Using <→> and <←> move this cursor to the position where you want a tab and press <f3>. You will see the symbol → appear in the ruler line. There will be one of these symbols for each (left) Tab setting.

To delete a (left) Tab setting, position the *ruler line* cursor over the Tab that you want to clear and press <[-]>.

Indent Tabs (↔)

Indent Tabs are not set up in the ruler line via the *Editing base layout* menu; they are just a special version of the (left) Tab.

Indent Tabs are displayed in your document as ↔. Indent Tabs enable you to indent the whole paragraph instead of just its first line while retaining the automatic word wrap facility. To do this move the cursor to the beginning of the first line of the paragraph and press <ALT>+<TAB>. This will cause the first line to indent just like the (left) Tab, but if you press <PARA>, or move the cursor to the next paragraph, you will find that LocoScript indents the whole paragraph.

3.3.2.4 - f4=Right tab (←) (*Editing base layout* menu option)

Right Tabs are represented in the ruler line by the ← symbol.

They allow you to
line up the right-hand edge
of a column like this.

They are set up in a similar way to (left) Tabs except that you press <f4> (i.e. <SHIFT>+<f3>). Right Tabs can be cleared by pressing <[-]>.

3.3.2.5 - f5=Centre tab (↔) (*Editing base layout* menu option)

Centre Tabs are represented in the ruler line by the ↔ symbol. They ensure that everything typed is centred around the Centre Tab. To use a Centre Tab while creating or editing a document press <TAB> to move the *character* cursor to the Centre Tab and then just type normally.

Then the
text that you type
will be centred
about the Centre Tab
like this.

Centre Tabs are set up in the ruler line via the *Editing base layout* menu by pressing <f5> and can be cleared by pressing <[-]>.

3.3.2.6 - f6=Decimal tab (*) (*Editing base layout* menu option)

Decimal tabs are represented in the ruler line by the * symbol. They ensure that the decimal points in a column of numbers are lined up. Integers (whole numbers) are positioned, as you would expect, to the left of the decimal point. For example:

    123.4
      0.1234
    1234
      .1234

Decimal Tabs are set up in the ruler line by pressing <f6> (i.e. <SHIFT>+<f5>) and can be cleared by pressing <[-]>.

The best way to see how these different tabs work is to

experiment with them. You will probably use the (left) Tab and
Indent Tab regularly, and the others less frequently.

It is important to realise that in addition to the Base
layout it is possible have any number of local layouts (99
maximum) in your document; each layout has a ruler line of its
own with (left) Tabs, Right Tabs, Centre Tabs and Decimal Tabs.
The method for adding extra layouts to your documents is
described in Chapter 3.3.6.1.

If you want to transfer tabulated text from one document
to another make sure that you set the tabs in the destination
document otherwise the layout of the destination document will
not correspond with that of the source document.

3.3.3 – *Editing base layout* menu (2nd line of Control zone)

If you look at the *Editing base layout* menu you will see that
its top line looks similar to this:

A:GRPNME/FILE.NME Editing base layout Printer Idle Using A: M:

The middle line shows a menu with 5 options:

⇒ Pitch ⇐   Line Pitch   Line Space   Italic   Justify

If you press <→> you will see the *menu* cursor move to the
right, like this:

   Pitch   ⇒ Line Pitch ⇐   Line Space   Italic   Justify

Each of the 5 options has various settings which can be
changed by pressing <[+]> or <[-]> when the *menu* cursor is
positioned over the option. Press <[+]> to increase (or set);
press <[-]> to decrease (or clear):

Pitch	Line Pitch	Line Space	Italic	Justify
PS	6	0		
PS D	8	½	⊗	⊗
10		1		
10 D		1½		
12		2		
12 D		2½		
15		3		
15 D				
17				
17 D				

3.3.3.1 - Pitch (Character pitch)
(*Editing base layout* menu option)

(Character) Pitch is the spacing of the characters (e.g. Pitch=12 means 12 characters will be printed per inch on a line; this is standard). D=double width characters, this halves the pitch, hence:

```
Pitch=10 D produces 5 characters per line inch
Pitch=12 D produces 6 characters per line inch
Pitch=15 D produces 7½ characters per line inch
Pitch=17 D produces 8½ characters per line inch
```

So the pitch can be varied between 5 and 17 characters per inch.

PS=proportionally spaced characters. Proportional spacing is a feature of word processors which causes the spacing between characters to be adjusted according to their width, in order to give a neater appearance to the text (e.g. i will take up less space than w). Punctuation is proportionally spaced, but numbers and spaces are not. The examples below show that Pitch=PS and Pitch=12 take up about the same length of line. In this paragraph Pitch=12, whereas generally in this book Pitch=PS.

Pitch=12 iiiiiiiiiiwwwwwwwwww

Pitch=PS iiiiiiiiiiwwwwwwwwww

The different character pitches don't show on the screen; LocoScript always *displays* a single character size. The full effect will not be seen until your document is printed out. However, LocoScript always shows correctly how many characters will fit between the margins and the actual line endings, as they will appear when printed.

```
                This is Pitch=17
               This is Pitch=15
              This is Pitch=PS
             This is Pitch=12
            This is Pitch=10
          This is Pitch=17 D
         This is Pitch=15 D
       This is Pitch=PS D
      This is Pitch=12 D
     This is Pitch=10 D
```

The current Pitch is shown in the second line of the Control zone (*Editing text* menu). For example :-:PiPS indicates

that the Base layout (global) Pitch=PS. Alternatively, :+:Pi17D
indicates that the cursor is positioned in a local layout with
Pitch=17D.

3.3.3.2 – Line Pitch (*Editing base layout* menu option)

Line Pitch is the number of lines LocoScript expects to print
per inch of the page length, and can be set to 6 or 8 lines
per inch. This is sometimes referred to as the *Base Line Pitch*,
in Amstrad's User Guide. In this paragraph Line Pitch=8,
whereas in the next paragraph it is 6.

The current Line Pitch is also shown in the Control zone.
For example :−:LP6 indicates Base layout Line Pitch=6.

3.3.3.3 – Line Space (*Editing base layout* menu option)

Line Space is equivalent to the lever which is provided on a
typewriter to enable you to adjust the line spacing. If you set
Line Space=2, then LocoScript will print your text with double
line spacing. The settings are 0, ½, 1, 1½, 2, 2½ or 3.

Line Space=0 so this line was re-printed
Line Space=½ relative to the line above
Line Space=1 relative to the line above

Line Space=1½ relative to the line above

Line Space=2 relative to the line above

Line Space=2½ relative to the line above

Line Space=3 relative to the line above

Line Space=0 can be used to good effect when using the
D=Direct Printing option of the *Disk management* menu (see
Chapter 4.4). You may find it helpful to set the line spacing
to 0 when filling in forms in order to be able to position
your lines of text accurately.

The current Line Space is shown in the Control zone. For
example :−:LS1 indicates Base layout Line Space=1.

3.3.3.4 – Italic (*Editing base layout* menu option)

Italic can be set on or off. A tick indicates that *Italic* is set
on and will result in a type-face with characters which slant
to the right, *like this*.

When Italic is set on *Italic* is displayed in the Control
zone.

3.3.3.5 - Justify (*Editing base layout* menu option)

Justify (justification) means the lining up of a column of text
on both the left and right-hand margins. With *Justify* off the
right-hand margin will be ragged. A tick indicates that *Justify*
is set on. This paragraph was printed with *Justify* off.

3.3.4 - *Editing header* menu

3.3.4.1 - f1=Layout (*Editing header* menu option)

This option is described in Chapter 3.3.2 and Chapter 3.3.3.

3.3.4.2 - Note that the *Editing header* menu does not have an f2 option.

3.3.4.3 - f3=Characters (*Editing header* menu option) ('0' or 'O' and '.' or ',')

If you press <f3> a pull-down menu like this will be displayed:

```
Characters:
⇥ Zero is 0     0 ⇤
  Zero is O
  Decimal is , 0
  Decimal is ,
```

This menu gives you two choices:

(1) either zero with a slash or zero without a slash
(2) either '.' (full stop (or period)) or ',' (comma)
used to align columns of numbers at a decimal tab.
The latter is often used in Europe.

Use <↓> and <↑> to position the *menu* cursor. Use <[+]> to
place a tick against your choice and then press <ENTER>.

3.3.4.4 - Note that the *Editing header* menu does not have an f4 option.

3.3.4.5 - f5=Tab count (*Editing header* menu option) (Layouts and Tabs)

Apart from the global Base layout, it is possible to have as
many as 99 other local layouts in your document. Each layout
can have as many as 99 tab stops. However, unless you really
need this many you are advised to restrict the number to about
ten because otherwise you will find your documents take up a

lot of disk space unnecessarily. To change the number of tabs (starting from the *Editing text* menu):

press <f7> to invoke the *Editor sub-menu* menu
press <ENTER> to select the *Edit Header* option
press <f7> to select *f7=Options*
press <f5> to select *f5=Tab count*

You will then see a pull-down menu similar to this:

Maxima:
99 layouts
99 tabs each

Change the settings to suit your requirements by pressing <↓> and then typing in the number that you want, followed by <ENTER>. Note that when you create a document the initial number of tab stops will be the same as set up in the TEMPLATE.STD document for that group.

3.3.4.6 – f6=Breaks (*Editing header* menu option) (Widows, orphans and broken paragraphs)

Pressing <f6> (i.e. <SHIFT>+<f5>) will invoke a pull-down menu similar to this:

Page breaks:

Widows & orphans
⇒ Prevented ● ⇐
Allowed

Broken paragraphs
Prevented
Allowed ●

This menu works like others; position the *menu* cursor using <↓> and <↑>, select your choice by pressing <[+]>.

This menu enables you to control the way LocoScript splits paragraphs between one page and the next. A paragraph that has all except its last line on one page is called a *widow*; if the last line is printed on the next page by itself, it is called an *orphan*. LocoScript automatically prevents these widows and orphans from occurring by breaking the page one line early, thus ensuring that there is always a minimum of two lines on the next page. You can override this by selecting the *Widows & orphans: Allowed* option.

If you want to prevent paragraphs from being split between two pages then select the *Broken paragraphs: Allowed* option. Place a tick alongside your choice and press <ENTER>.

If you prevent the occurrence of broken paragraphs then you don't need to worry about widows and orphans!

3.3.4.7 – f7=Page size (*Editing header* menu option) (Headers and Footers)

Pressing <f7> invokes a menu like this:

        Page size:

        Page length 60

        Header zone 8
         position   6

        ⋏ page body 47

        Footer zone 5
         position   56

When you change the size of paper that you are using there are two things you must do:

        (1) set up the *Printer Options* menu (refer to Chapter 4)
        (2) set up the *Page size* menu (this is described here)

To set up the *Page size* menu five parameters are needed:

        (1) Page length (number of lines)
        (2) Header zone (number of lines)
        (3) Header text position (number of lines from the top of the page)
        (4) Footer zone (number of lines)
        (5) Footer text position (number of lines from the top of the page)

The values that are shown are measured in terms of the number of lines in the document's base line pitch which is explained in Chapter 3.3.3.2. The *base* line pitch is the line pitch of the Base layout.

If your paper is 1 inch long then with a base line pitch of 6 you can print 6 lines on it, if your paper is 5 inches

long then the paper length is 30 lines (5x6=30), and so on.
Hence the paper length for A5=50, 11 inch = 66 and A4 = 70.

The *Header zone* is the top margin between the top edge of
the paper and where the page body begins. Similarly the *Footer
zone* is the bottom margin between the bottom of the page body
and the bottom edge of the paper. Neither of these zones is
displayed when you edit a document; they are normally only
seen when you print the document. You can put text into either
of these zones. One possible use is to have the title of a
document or report in the *Header zone*, and a page number and
date in the *Footer zone*. The setting up of Header and Footer
text is described in Chapter 3.3.5.

Page length = Header zone + page body + Footer zone.

When you use single sheet stationery there must be at
least 6 lines between the top of the paper and the header text
position, consequently the Header zone itself must be 6 lines
or more. The Footer must be at least 3 lines; if you have
footer text then there must be at least 3 lines below this
text.

The default settings, when you load LocoScript, are for a
Header zone of 9 lines and a Footer zone of 7 lines. Hence,
unless you set up Header text the first 9 lines will be blank.
Similarly with the last 7 lines. The text of your document will
appear on the remaining 54 lines.

The Header (or Footer) text position doesn't have to be
located within the Header (or Footer) zone if you don't want it
to be; if it isn't though, you risk losing the spacing between
the Header (or Footer) text and the page body.

If you want to have Footer text such as 'continues'
printed immediately below the page body then set:

Footer text position = Header zone + page body + 1.

Before printing a document for the first time, you should
check that the *Gap length* is less than the difference between
the Page length and the Footer text position. To check the Gap
length you will need to use the *Printer options* menu (refer to
Chapter 4 if you need instructions on how to do this).

As you make changes to the five parameters, LocoScript
automatically calculates the size of the page body for you. If
you try to make the page body = 0 then LocoScript will report
the inconsistency.

LocoScript enables you to produce correctly paginated draft versions of a document on continuous stationery without having to alter the *Page size* parameters which have already been set up for single sheet stationery. The single sheet stationery must not be more than one inch longer than the continuous stationery. If your single sheet stationery is A4 size then 11-inch continuous stationery is good enough. However, you will still have to set up the printer correctly when you change the stationery.

The current cursor position is displayed in the Control zone during editing, as for example *line 3 of 47*.

3.3.4.8 - f8=Pagination (*Editing header* menu option)

Press <f8> (i.e. <SHIFT>+<f7>) to invoke this menu:

```
Pagination
→ First page number    1 ↔
  All pages same        ⊕
  First page differs
  Last page differs
  Odd/even pages differ
  First page
    Header enabled
    Footer enabled  ⊕
  Last page
    Header enabled
    Footer enabled  ⊕
```

You can change the first page that you want your document to start from by typing the new page number (maximum 9999) and pressing <ENTER>. The current page number is displayed in the Control zone during editing a document, for example *Page 112*.

Select *the First page differs* option when you want the first page of the document to be different from all the others. For example the first page of a memorandum would normally differ from the continuation pages.

Select the *Last page differs* option when for example you want to have 'continued' printed on all pages except the last.

Select *the Odd/even pages differ option* when you want the text to differ, as for example the page numbers in a book.

If your document is a chapter in a book then you might

only want to have the Footer text on the first page but both
the Header and Footer texts on all the following pages. So put
a tick against:

> *First page : Footer enabled*
> *Last page : Header enabled*
> *Last page : Footer enabled.*

3.3.5 – *Editing pagination* menu

Setting up Header and Footer text

LocoScript enables you to set up text in the Header and/or
Footer zones. To be able to do this you will need to display
the *Editing pagination* menu. From the *Editing text* menu press
⟨f7⟩ to display the *Editor sub-modes* menu and press ⟨ENTER⟩
to select the *Edit header* option. If the *character* cursor is
not already at the top of the screen then LocoScript will move
it to the top and then after a short delay, display the *Editing
pagination* menu.

What you see depends on how the *Pagination* menu (the
f8=Pagination option of the *Editing header* menu) has been set
up and whether or not some text has already been typed in. The
screen is always divided into four zones:

> header 1
> footer 1
> header 2
> footer 2

If some Header and Footer text has already been set up
then it will be displayed.

There are messages incorporated in the lines that divide
up the screen, which tell you how the text in each section will
be used.

If the *All pages same* option in the *Pagination* menu has
been selected then you will see the following:

> _____end of header 1 : used for all pages_____
> _____end of footer 1 : used for all pages_____
> _____end of header 2 : used for no pages at all_____
> _____end of footer 2 : used for no pages at all_____

If the *First page differs* option in the *Pagination* menu

has been selected then you will see the following:

```
_____end of header 1 ; used for only the first page_____
_____end of footer 1 ; used for only the first page_____
_____end of header 2 ; used for all pages except the first_____
_____end of footer 2 ; used for all pages except the first_____
```

If the *Last page differs* option in the *Pagination* menu has been selected then you will see the following:

```
_____end of header 1 ; used for all pages except the last_____
_____end of footer 1 ; used for all pages except the last_____
_____end of header 2 ; used only for the last page_____
_____end of footer 2 ; used only for the last page_____
```

If the *Odd/even pages differ* option in the *Pagination* menu has been selected then you will see the following:

```
_____end of header 1 ; used for all odd pages_____
_____end of footer 1 ; used for all odd pages_____
_____end of header 2 ; used for all even pages_____
_____end of footer 2 ; used for all even pages_____
```

Text that is placed in these zones is not displayed while you are editing your document. The only time that the Header and Footer zone text is displayed is when you invoke the *Edit pagination* menu to edit the text (or in order to select f7=Options which leads to the *Editing base layout* menu).

If you want to see a few examples of Header and Footer text just load in one of the 12 documents that Amstrad have provided, from the group called TEMPLATE. For example load in the document called MEMO and have a look at its Header and Footer text by pressing <f7> followed by <ENTER>, from the *Editing text* menu.

Text held in the Header and Footer zones is not affected by any of the word processor codes that are used in the main document itself. These codes are temporarily suspended while the Footer text is printed at the bottom of one page and the Header text is printed at the top of the other. The document then continues to be printed with any layout differences of its own (either global Base layout or local layout differences).

Conversely, none of the word processing codes that are set up in the Header and/or Footer zones affect the main document itself.

If you type text into the *header 2* or *footer 2* zones when

the *All pages same* option is selected then this text will not
be used. If you alter the setting in the *Pagination* menu (e.g.
from *All pages same* to *Odd/even pages differ*) the text will
remain unchanged but this time it will be used for the even
numbered pages.

Setting up Header and Footer text is similar to editing a
document, insofar as you can use the embedded control
commands. However, you are limited to using the Base layout.

When you have finished setting up the Header and Footer
text press <EXIT> to invoke a menu like this:

         Exit pagination editing:
  ⇥ ● Use this pagination   ↤
     Recover old pagination
     Empty pagination text
     Abandon edit altogether

Use this pagination (*Exit pagination editing* menu option)

Press <ENTER> to select this option and after a short delay
the display will return to the *Editing text* menu.

Recover old pagination (*Exit pagination editing* menu option)

If you have started to make a change to the Header or Footer
text and decide that you want to abandon the change, press <↓>
to move the *menu* cursor down to this option and then press
<ENTER>. The original Header and Footer text will be returned
intact.

WARNING - If you start without any Header or
Footer text (e.g. when creating a new document), type some in
and then select this option, LocoScript will efficiently recover
the original pagination for you i.e. nothing!

Empty pagination text (*Exit pagination editing* menu option)

If you want to clear the existing Header and Footer text in
order to replace it with something else, press <↓> to move the
menu cursor down to this option and press <ENTER>.

WARNING - If you change your mind after clearing
all the text like this, you will not be able to recover it by
selecting the *Recover old pagination* option. If you find
yourself in this situation choose the *Abandon edit altogether*
option, and start again. That way the original Header and
Footer text will be restored (assuming that you have

previously saved the document at least once and are not
creating it for the first time).

Abandon edit altogether (*Exit pagination editing* menu option)

If you want to select this option move the *menu* cursor down to
cover it using <↓> and then press <ENTER>. When you select
this option LocoScript returns to the *Disk management* menu
and all the changes that have been made to the Header and/or
Footer zones as well as the document itself, since starting the
current edit, are destroyed.

Page numbering

Apart from text, for example, like the chapter headings and
book title in the Header and Footer zones, it is possible to
get LocoScript to number the pages of your document for you,
automatically.

There are two things that you have to do:

(1) insert a special control code in the text
(2) tell LocoScript how much space to allow for the
number

Press <f6> to invoke the *Page layout* menu (this menu is
described in more detail in Chapter 3.3.5.6. Move the *menu*
cursor to select the option called *this Page Number*; pressing
<ENTER> will insert the control code (PageNo) in the text.
Don't forget that if you want to be able to see codes you must
have a tick set against the *Codes* option of the *Show* menu (see
Chapter 3.3.5.1.

Of course, you can place the (PageNo) code either in the
Header zone or in the Footer zone, depending on whether you
want the page number to be printed at the top or bottom of the
page.

Next choose one of three possible symbols. The symbols
are:

< if you want the number to be positioned to the
left
> if you want the number to be positioned to the
right
= if you want the number to be centred

You need to type one of these characters for every digit
in the maximum page number. For example, if the highest page

number is going to be 99 (i.e. two digits) then you must type
<< or >> or ==. Alternatively, if the highest page number is
going to be 999 (i.e. three digits) then you must type <<< or
>>> or ===. If you don't do this and have placed, for example,
just one symbol > in the header and try to print page 103 then
the result will be 3; the 10 will not be printed. It goes
without saying that these symbols must be placed in the same
zone as the (PageNo) code, following it.

If you want the page number to be preceded by the word
'Page' and printed at the top of each page, then you must also
type the word 'Page' in the Header text before you insert the
(PageNo) code. Normally you would insert the (RJust) control
code before the word 'Page' in the Header text in order to
justify the word 'Page' to the right hand end on the odd
numbered pages. Use the *Lines* menu to insert the (RJust) code
(see Chapter 3.4). That is assuming that you have selected the
Odd/even pages differ option from the *Pagination* menu.

Alternatively, if you want the page number to be centred
at the bottom of the page between a pair of hyphens like this:

           - 1 - , - 2 - , - 103 - , etc.

then you will need to place a (Centre) control code in the
Footer text before typing the first hyphen, then the (PageNo)
code. So the Footer text would look like this if the maximum
page number were 999:

           (Centre)- (PageNo)=== -

Of course, if you haven't placed a tick against the *Codes*
option of the *Show* menu then the Footer text would look like
this:

           - === -

If you have selected the *Odd/even pages differ* option
from the *Pagination* menu then don't forget to set up similar
text for the even numbered pages by typing the same thing in
the Footer 2 zone.

LocoScript also enables you to number the pages of your
document as, for example, Page 1 of 17, Page 2 of 17, etc. (in a
document that has 17 pages). Of course, if your document
comprises a different number of pages that will be taken care
of; LocoScript automatically adjusts the last number to match
the total number of pages!

To get LocoScript to do this you need to add another code followed by the group of location symbols again. Select f6=Pages to invoke the *Page layout* menu, then move the *menu* cursor down to the *Last Page Number* option and press <ENTER> to insert the (LPageNo) code. So the Footer zone would look like this:

(Centre)Page (PageNo)=== of (LPageNo)===

3.3.5.1 - f1=Show (*Editing pagination* menu option)

This option is the same as the f1 option in the *Editing text* menu which is mentioned briefly in Chapter 3.2.2 and Chapter 3.2.3. It is explained more fully in Chapter 3.3.6.1.

3.3.5.2 - Note that there is no f2 option in the *Editing pagination* menu

3.3.5.3 - f3=Emphasis (*Editing pagination* menu option)

This option is the same as the f3 option in the *Editing text* menu and is described in Chapter 3.4.1.3.

3.3.5.4 - f4=Style (*Editing pagination* menu option)

This option is the same as the f4 option in the *Editing text* menu and is described in Chapter 3.4.1.4.

3.3.5.5 - f5=Lines (*Editing pagination* menu option)

This option is the same as the f5 option in the *Editing text* menu and is described in Chapter 3.4.1.5.

3.3.5.6 - f6=Pages (*Editing pagination* menu option)

This option is the same as the f6 option in the *Editing text* menu and is described in Chapter 3.4.1.6.

3.3.5.7 - f7=Options (*Editing pagination* menu option)

Select this option to invoke the *Editing header* menu. See Chapter 3.3.4.

3.3.5.8 - f8=Blocks (*Editing pagination* menu option)

This option is the same as the f8 option in the *Editing text* menu and is described in Chapter 3.2.4.

3.3.6 – *Editing text* menu
      (Making local changes to the layout)

3.3.6.1 – f1=Show (*Editing text* menu option)

Press <f1> to invoke a pull-down menu like this:

```
        Show state of:
      → Codes          ←
        Rulers
        Blanks
        Spaces
        Effectors
```

        Use the <↓> and <↑> keys to position the *menu* cursor and
<[+]> to set a tick against the option(s) of your choice (you
can place a tick against as many as you want). Use <[-]> if
you want to clear a tick that is already there. When you have
set the combination that you want press <ENTER>.

        The current state of the settings will be saved with the
document so that when you next load the document back into the
PCW's memory they will be automatically restored. The Codes
and/or Rulers and/or Blanks and/or Spaces and/or Effectors
will be displayed only if set; they cannot be printed.

        With LocoScript, the line endings that are displayed on
the screen are the line endings that you will get when the
document is printed; what you see is what you get. Therefore,
it makes sense to preview your document by moving the
character cursor from the top to the bottom of the document,
(with all of these settings clear of ticks) immediately before
printing a document. Doing this will show you what your
document will look like when it is printed, without the
distracting clutter of these codes.

Codes (*Show* menu option)

If you select this option then all the word processing codes in
the document will be displayed. You will find that lines which
contain codes become longer to accommodate the codes but the
line endings will remain unaffected. You will probably want
this option set most of the time, particularly when inserting
word processing codes using the other *Editing text* menu
options.

Rulers (*Show* menu option)

If you select this option then any local ruler lines that have been set up within the document will be displayed immediately above the first line that they affect. You will probably only want this option set when creating local layouts.

Blanks (*Show* menu option)

If you set this option then any places in the document where nothing has been typed will be shown as dots. You will probably not use this feature very frequently. However, it can be useful when creating tables to help your eye scan across the screen to avoid skipping a line either up or down.

Spaces (*Show* menu option)

If you set this option then any places where spaces have been typed using the <SPACE BAR> will be displayed as tiny triangles. This feature can be useful for checking the spacing between words, particularly when *Justify* is set on (see Chapter 3.3.3.5). Otherwise you will probably find it more convenient not to have these spaces highlighted like this, as it tends to clutter up the screen.

Effectors (*Show* menu option)

If you set this option then all carriage returns (resulting from pressing <RETURN>), tabs (including Indent Tabs), and the 'End page here' symbols will be displayed. You will probably find it useful to have this option set on most of the time; it's a pity that it isn't located at the top of the menu!

3.3.6.2 - f2=Layout (*Editing text* menu option)
(Making local changes to the layout)

Insert Layout (*Document layout* menu option)
Brand New layout

Creating a brand new layout within a document

LocoScript doesn't just limit you to the single Base layout in your documents. You can have a maximum of 99 different local layouts. Of course, it is also possible to have more than one layout in TEMPLATE.STD itself, as it is a document.

In order to create a document with space for a photograph, in the middle on the left-hand side, you can still make use of the Base layout at the top and bottom of the document. However, you will need a layout with the left-hand margin indented to make space for the photograph. You will also need some text for the upper section; anything typed in

will do, provided that it is at least a few lines in length.
You could insert a block of text that you have saved from
READ.ME. Refer to Chapter 3.2.4.1 if you can't remember how to
do this. When you have created a document with some text in it,
save it on disk by pressing <EXIT> and then <ENTER>.

To be able to place the photograph in your document, you
will need to add another layout. In practice it is unlikely
that you would want to change the Base layout in TEMPLATE.STD
just for the sake of a photograph in one document, as not
every document might have a photograph. So you should create
an additional layout for your new document and not
TEMPLATE.STD.

From the Disk management menu press <E> followed by
<ENTER> to load your document back into memory so that you
can edit it. Next, move the cursor to the point from which you
want the new layout to take effect; in this case move the
cursor to the bottom of your document, as you want the
existing text to be the top section of the final document.
Press <f1>, to invoke the Show menu, and check that there are
ticks against both the Codes and Rulers options, in the Show
menu, to ensure that your new layout will be displayed on the
screen. Next, press <f2> (i.e. <SHIFT>+<f1>) in order to invoke
the Layout menu:

         Document layout:

         Insert Layout
      → brand New layout ←
         Layout   ??
         Base layout

         Edit Layout
         layout ??

You are going to create a new layout for your document,
so press <ENTER> to select the brand New Layout option. When
you do this LocoScript will display Editing layout followed by
a layout number, in the Control zone. If you haven't already
created a new layout in this document then the layout number
will be 1. Notice that the Control zone now resembles the
Editing base layout menu described in Chapter 3.3.2.

Invoke the ruler line cursor by pressing <↓> and then by
pressing <→>, move it to cover the number 5. If the cursor
overshoots the number 5, you can always move it back by
pressing <←>. When the cursor is over the number 5, press <f1>
to reset the left-hand margin, then press <EXIT> to return to
your document.

You should now be able to see a code like this
(:+:LayouT1) displayed on the screen together with the new
ruler line.

The *brand New layout* option is only displayed when there
are still some unallocated layouts remaining. If you have
allocated all the available layouts then you will have to
increase the number. The maximum number of layouts that you
can allocate in a particular document is determined by the
number that has been set up as being available in the *Tab
count* menu (see Chapter 3.3.4.5).

You can use the same layout more than once in the same
document.

Note that when the cursor is within the local layout the
Control zone displays the layout number. For example,
:+:Layout1. When you move the cursor outside the local layout
the Control zone reverts to the Base layout (i.e. :-:Layout).

Insert Layout (*Document layout* menu option)
Layout ??

This option is used to insert specific *layout* codes. To use it
move the menu cursor to this option, press <ENTER> followed by
the number of the layout that you want to use. Note that an
additional return character is inserted, this can be deleted if
it is not needed.

LocoScript allows you to insert codes for layouts which
don't exist. Sometimes this is useful as you can insert layout
codes and then define their layouts later; when you do this
LocoScript goes through your document making the necessary
changes automatically.

You can check to see whether or not a layout exists by
attempting to edit the layout; if the layout resembles the Base
layout then you know that it doesn't exist. An alternative is
to always use the *brand New layout* option, in which case
LocoScript will always allocate the next available number to
the new layout.

Insert Layout (*Document layout* menu option)
Base layout

You will need to type some text to fill the middle section (i.e.
below the new ruler line). When you have done that, move the
cursor to the bottom of the document and press <f2> again.
This time move the *menu* cursor down to *Base layout* and then

press <ENTER>. Notice that LocoScript puts another ruler line in your document together with the *Base layout* code (:-:LayouT). Now everything that is typed in will once again have the same format as the top section; the margins will be the same as the upper section of the document.

Whenever you insert a local layout code in your document that layout applies until you insert the *Base layout* code to turn it off.

Edit Layout (*Document layout* menu option)
Current layout

Document layout:

Insert Layout
⇥ brand New layout ⇤
Layout   ??
Base layout

Edit Layout
current layout
layout ??

This option enables you to edit the current layout. The *current* layout is the layout that the *character* cursor was in when you invoked this menu. This option is only displayed when the *character* cursor is located in a part of the document that is controlled by a local layout; it is not displayed when the cursor is in a section that is governed by the Base layout. If there is no local layout in force then the Base layout applies, by default. To edit the Base layout refer to Chapter 3.3.2.

Edit Layout (*Document layout* menu option)
Layout ??

This option enables you to edit a layout by specifying its number. Select the option using the *menu* cursor, type the number and press <ENTER>. The changes that you make will only affect those areas of the document which use that layout.

3.4 - ADDING A BIT OF STYLE

3.4.1 - *Editing text* menu

3.4.1.1 - f1=Show (*Editing text* menu option)

This option is described in Chapter 3.3.6.1.

3.4.1.2 – f2=Layout (*Editing text* menu option)

This option is described in Chapter 3.3.6.2.

3.4.1.3 – f3=Emphasis (*Editing text* menu option)

Press <f3> to invoke a pull-down menu like this:

Emphasis codes:
→ :-: Underline   ←
  :-: Bold
  :-: Double
  :-: ReVerse Video

If you want to underline some text in your document then press
<[+]> and the pull-down menu will extend further like this:

Emphasis codes:
  :+: Underline
→ Full underline   ● ←
  Word underline
  :-: Bold
  :-: Double
  :-: ReVerse Video

Full underline (*Emphasis* menu option)

Both the words and the spaces between them will be
underlined. The underlining will be displayed and printed.

Press <ENTER> to insert the set underline code (:+:UL) in
your document at the position that the cursor occupied before
you invoked the menu. Move the *character* cursor to the point
in your text where you want the underlining to end and press
<f3> to invoke the menu again (which will still be in its
extended form). Press <[-]> and the menu will shrink back to
its original size.

Press <ENTER> to insert the clear underline code (:-:UL).
If you don't place the clear underline code in your text (or if
you accidentally delete it), then LocoScript will appear to go
beserk underlining everything after the set underline code. To
recover from this situation replace the clear underline code
where it should be in your text and either move the *character*
cursor down or press <RELAY> to tidy up the display.

If you feel that the lines produced are too close to the
text you could, for example, set the line pitch to 8 and the
line space to ½ and then put a row of underlined spaces below
the text.

If you are not satisfied with the standard method of underlining text and you want double or even triple underlining then you can have it; with LocoScript almost anything is possible! While this is not available as a control code, by using a combination of = or ≡ (i.e. <SHIFT>+<ALT>) and varying the character pitch and the line space it is possible to produce some passable results.

Word underline (*Emphasis* menu option)

If you want LocoScript to underline only the words and not the spaces, then press <f3> to invoke the menu and press <[+]> to extend it. Then press <↓> once to move the *menu* cursor down to the *Word underline* option. Press <[+]> to set the tick against the *Word underline* option and finally press <ENTER> to insert the (:+:Wordul) code in your document at the position that the cursor occupied before you invoked the menu.

Move the *character* cursor to end of the last word that you want to be underlined and press <f3> to invoke the menu again (which will still be in in its extended form. Press <[-]> and the menu will shrink back to its original size again. Press <ENTER> to insert the clear underline code (:-:UL).

Note that you can get LocoScript to underline parts of words by positioning the cursor on a character and setting the (:+:Wordul) code and then moving the cursor to another character and inserting the (:-:UL) code. While the codes split the word on the screen it will not be split when it is printed because codes themselves are never printed. If you want to see it without the codes, all you have to do is clear the tick from the *Codes* option of the *Show* menu.

Bold (*Emphasis* menu option)

Use <↓> to move the *menu* cursor over the *:-: Bold* option and press <[+]> followed by <ENTER>. Doing this will insert a (:+:Bold) code in the document at the position that the cursor occupied before you invoked the menu. Subsequent characters will be printed in a heavier **bold** type for special emphasis. Bold characters are not shown on the screen.

When you want to want to return to the normal type press <f3> to invoke the *Emphasis* menu again, move the *menu* cursor to the *:+: Bold* option and press <[-]> to clear the setting. Finally press <ENTER> to insert the (:-:Bold) code in the text. Alternatively, you could press <[+]>, <B> and then <[-]>, <B> (please see Chapter 3.5.3).

When the cursor is positioned over a bold character *Bold* is displayed in the second line of the Control zone in the *Editing text* menu.

Double (*Emphasis* menu option)

To select this option move the *menu* cursor down to cover it and press ⟨[+]⟩ and then ⟨ENTER⟩. The (:+:Double) code will then be inserted in the document and this puts the printer into its Double-strike mode.

All subsequent characters will be *Double* printed until you insert the (:-:Double) code by pressing ⟨f3⟩ once and ⟨↓⟩ twice, followed by ⟨ENTER⟩. The characters on the screen will not be affected; the effect will only be seen when the document is printed.

If you select the *High quality* option from the printer *Options* menu (see Chapter 4 if you are not familiar with using this menu) and use *Double* print codes in your text then the result will be similar to using the *Bold* print code. In fact *Bold* and *Double* print are virtually indistinguishable. The *High quality* option is sometimes called Near Letter Quality or NLQ because a good quality of print is produced by the printer making a second pass.

However, if you select the *Draft quality* option from the printer *Options* menu and use *Double* print codes in your text then it will be printed in a different type which is sans-serif. Sans-serif is a style of printing type with no serifs, which are the fine line projections which extend from the main stroke of a character. When *Double* print codes are used this way it is also possible to distinguish between *Bold* and *Double* print.

When Pitch=15 or Pitch=17 the Bold or Double control codes are only effective when printing in draft quality, because the pins in the printhead are not small enough to make text look any bolder without looking smudged.

ReVerse Video (*Emphasis* menu option)

Select this option in the same sort of way by using ⟨↓⟩, ⟨[+]⟩ and ⟨ENTER⟩ to insert the (:+:Rev) code.

Use ⟨↓⟩, ⟨[-]⟩ and ⟨ENTER⟩ to insert the (:-:Rev) code when you want the display to return to normal.

Text between these codes will be displayed in reverse video (i.e. highlighted) on the screen but text that is printed will not be affected.

3.4.1.4 - f4=Style (*Editing text* menu option)

Pressing ⟨f4⟩ (i.e. ⟨SHIFT⟩+⟨f3⟩) invokes a menu like this:

```
        Character style:
    ⊅ :-: Half Height  ⊱
      :-: Italic
      ;-; Pitch     PS
```

The pitch that is displayed in the last option will depend on the current Base layout pitch of your document; in this example the pitch is proportional spacing (PS).

Half Height (*Style* menu option)

If you press ⟨[+]⟩ the pull-down menu will extend further like this:

```
        Character style:
      :+: Half Height
    ⊅ SupeRscript    ⊖ ⊱
      SuBscript
      :-: Italic
      ;-; Pitch     PS
```

SupeRscript (*Style* menu option)

Press ⟨ENTER⟩ to insert the (:+:SupeR) code in your document. This causes all subsequent characters to be printed in a half height raised (i.e. superscript) type. This effect is not displayed on the screen.

To return to normal type press ⟨f4⟩, then ⟨[-]⟩ followed by ⟨ENTER⟩ to insert the (:-:SupeR) code in the text.

SuBscript (*Style* menu option)

To obtain subscripted type press ⟨↓⟩ to move the *menu* cursor down to the *SuBscript* option and press ⟨[+]⟩ to set the tick against this option, then press ⟨ENTER⟩ to insert the (:+:SuB) code in the text. This effect is not displayed on the screen.

To return to normal type press ⟨f4⟩, then ⟨[-]⟩ followed

by <ENTER> to insert the (:-:SuB) code in the text.

THIS IS SupeRscript and THIS IS SuBscript.

Italic (*Style* menu option)

Select this option to obtain *italic* print for emphasis. This effect is not displayed on the screen. Move the *menu* cursor down to this option, press <[+]> followed by <ENTER> to insert the italic code (:+:Italic) in the text.

To return to normal type move the cursor down to this option, press <[-]> followed by <ENTER>.

When the cursor is positioned over an italicised character the word *Italic* is displayed in the Control zone.

Pitch (*Style* menu option)

If you move the *menu* cursor down to this option and press <[+]> then the menu will extend down further like this:

```
Character style:
:+: Half Height
SupeRscript     @
SuBscript
:-: Italic
:+: Pitch      PS
10 Pitch
12 Pitch
15 Pitch
17 Pitch
↳ Prop. spacing  @ ↵
normal width    @
Double width
```

Note that LocoScript places the *menu* cursor over the Base layout pitch (in this example it is *Prop. spacing*). To change the pitch move the *menu* cursor to the pitch that you require and press <[+]>. The *:+: Pitch* option will change to match your choice. If you want the characters to be double width then also move the *menu* cursor down to the *Double width* option and press <[+]> to set the tick. Next press <ENTER> to insert the pitch code in the text. For example (:+:Pitch15).

When you insert a new pitch code (either *Normal* width code or *Double* width) it automatically cancels any previous code that has been inserted in the text.

To return to the Base layout pitch press <f4> and move the cursor to the :+: Pitch and press <[-]> followed by <ENTER>. Doing this will insert the (:-:Pitch) code.

3.4.1.5 - f5=Lines (*Editing text* menu option)

Press <f5> to invoke a pull-down menu like this:

```
          Line layout:
        ≑ Centre line          ∈
          Right Justify line
          insert soft space
          insert hard space
          insert soft hyphen
          insert hard hyphen
          Line Spacing    ??
          Line Pitch       ?
```

You can select an option from this menu by moving the *menu* cursor to cover it and then pressing <ENTER>. In the case of the last two options you need to type a number before pressing <ENTER>.

Centre line (*Lines* menu option)

Select this option to insert the (Centre) code in your text. Text between this position and the next end of line, tab, end of page symbol or right justify code, will be centred on the page. The text will be displayed as well as printed centred.

Right Justify line (*Lines* menu option)

Select this option to insert the (RJust) code in your text. Text between this position and the next end of line, end of page, or centre code will be positioned on the page so that the last character of the line is in line with the right-hand margin. This will be displayed as well as printed.

Insert soft space (*Lines* menu option)

Select this option to insert a code which allows a space to show only if an end of line wraparound occurs at this point.

Insert hard space (*Lines* menu option)

Select this option to insert a code that produces a space between two words that shows and which cannot be broken by end of line wraparound.

Insert soft hyphen (*Lines* menu option)

Select this option to insert a code which allows a hyphen to show only if an end of line wraparound occurs at this point.

Insert hard hyphen (*Lines* menu option)

Select this option to insert a code that produces a hyphen between two words that shows and which cannot be broken by end of line wraparound.

Line Spacing (*Lines* menu option)

Select this option to change the line spacing. You will need to type 0, ½, 1, 1½, 2, 2½ or 3 before pressing <ENTER>. The code that is inserted takes effect from the end of the current line. The normal setting is 1. Line Space is described in Chapter 3.3.3.3.

Line Pitch (*Lines* menu option)

Select this option to change the line pitch. You will need to type either 6 or 8 before pressing <ENTER>. The normal setting is 6. Line Pitch is described in Chapter 3.3.3.2.

3.4.1.6 - f6=Pages (*Editing text* menu option)

Press <f6> to invoke a pull-down menu like this:

```
          Page layout:
      ⇥ end page here          ⇤
        Last Line of page
        Keep lines together
          Above              ??
          Below              ??
        insert page number
          this Page Number
          Last Page Number
```

End page here (*Page layout* menu option)

Select this option to force an early page break by pressing <ENTER>. The character that the *character* cursor was on before you invoked this pull-down menu will become the first character of the new page. When you invoke a pull-down menu like this the *character* cursor temporarily disappears from the text on the screen, so you need to make a mental note of its position before invoking the menu.

Word processing codes like this can be deleted; you may
need to press <RELAY> to tidy up the display if you do this.
The *end page here* code takes priority over any *Keep* codes that
have already been inserted in the text.

Last Line of page (*Page layout* menu option)

Use this option to mark a line as the last line of the page.
The next line in the document will become the first line of the
next page. This code takes priority over any *Keep* codes that
have already been inserted in the document.

Pressing <ALT>+<RETURN> does exactly the same thing; it
inserts an end of page code in your text and forces a page
break to occur.

Keep lines together (*Page layout* menu option)
Above ??

Use this option to insert a code to ensure that a particular
number of lines above the current position of the *character*
cursor will not be affected by a natural page break. When you
count the lines make sure that you include the current line.

Keep lines together (*Page layout* menu option)
Below ??

This option allows you to insert a code to ensure that a
particular number of lines below the current position of the
character cursor will not be affected by a natural page break.
When you count the lines make sure that you include the
current line.

Insert this page number (*Page layout* menu option)
This Page Number

Use this option to insert the code that precedes the symbols
(i.e. a number of <'s, >'s or ='s) that are used to mark where
you want the number of the current page to be positioned.

Insert this page number (*Page layout* menu option)
Last Page Number

Select this option to insert the code that precedes the
symbols (i.e. a number of <'s, >'s or ='s) that are used to mark
where you want the number of the last page of the document to
be positioned.

3.4.1.7 - f7=Modes (*Editing text* menu option)

This option is described in Chapter 3.2.4.1 and Chapter 3.3.2.

3.4.1.8 - f8=Blocks (*Editing text* menu option)

This option is described in Chapter 3.2.4.

3.5 - BY-PASSING MENUS

3.5.1 - Using the Set and Clear menus

While LocoScript provides lots of pull-down menus to help you to use its various word processing features these are really intended for the beginner. After you have used LocoScript for a while you will probably find the need to keep invoking these separate menus a nuisance.

LocoScript therefore provides a quicker way of putting the relevant codes into your text by means of the *Set* and *Clear* menus. You can think of these menus as being condensed versions of the individual menus. As you might expect, the *Set* menu is used to insert the codes that set a function and the *Clear* menu is used to insert the codes that clear a function.

Press <[+]> to invoke the *Set* menu or press <[-]> to invoke the *Clear* menu. You will find that there will be a short delay before the menus appear; if you press <[+]> or <[-]> followed by <[≡]> (i.e. the key between <←> and <→>) the menu will be displayed immediately:

```
+!_____          -!_____
↔ Bold           ←          ↔ Bold           ←
  Centre                      Double
  Double                      Italic
  Italic                      Keep         ??
  Keep         ??             LayouT
  LayouT       ??             Line Pitch
  Line Pitch    ?             Line Spacing
  Line Spacing ??             Pitch
  Last Line                   ReVerse
  Last Page Number            SuBscript
  Pitch       ?? ?            SupeRscript
  Page Number                 UnderLine
  ReVerse                     ( ) soft space
  Right Justify               (-) soft hyphen
  SuBscript
  SupeRscript
  UnderLine
  Word underline
  UniT
    hard space
  - hard hyphen
```

These menus are used in much the same sort of way as the
others, use the cursor control keys to position the *menu* cursor
over the option that you want to select.

The options with question marks after them (e.g. Keep ??
which is explained in Chapter 3.3.5.6) require a number to be
typed before you press <ENTER>. With others (e.g. Pitch ?? ?)
once you have typed the number (e.g. 12) then by pressing <[+]>
or <[-]> you can increment or decrement the value until it is
to your liking and then press <ENTER>.

As soon as you press <ENTER> the code will be inserted
in the text at the position last occupied by the cursor before
you invoked the menu; the menu will then disappear. If you want
to insert another code then you will have to invoke the *Set* or
Clear menu again.

Once you get to know the various word processing
functions you will find it much quicker to use these menus; get
into the habit of using them as soon as you can.

3.5.2 - Using abbreviations

When you become an experienced user of LocoScript you might
find moving menu cursors up and down a bit tedious. In fact
you don't have to move them using the cursor control keys at
all. You will probably have noticed that certain letters in the
menu options and codes are capitals; these letters can be used
as abbreviations for the codes. All you have to do is type in
any abbreviated form that includes the capital letters.

Note that you must include the capital letters and that
this works for any of the pull-down menus.

To try this feature invoke the *Set* menu by pressing <[+]>
followed by <[≡]>. Suppose you want to insert the last page
number code. Press <L> and you will see the menu shrink so
that it just contains all the options that start with L. Press
<P> and the menu will shrink again to show just *Line Pitch* ?
and *Last Page Number*. Press <N> and the menu reduces to *Last
Page Number*. Press <ENTER> if you want to insert the (LPageNo)
code, otherwise press <CAN>.

3.5.3 - Avoiding menus altogether

If you don't want to use the pull-down menus you don't have to;
LocoScript allows you to by-pass them altogether. To do this

just press ⟨[+]⟩ and immediately type the abbreviation. Your abbreviation must contain the capital letters shown in the *Set* and *Clear* menus. For example, if you want to insert the ⟨Centre⟩ code just press ⟨[+]⟩ and then ⟨C⟩.

You must type enough of a code for LocoScript to be able to recognise it. For example if you press ⟨L⟩ and ⟨P⟩, LocoScript will not insert the ⟨LPageNo⟩ code until you press ⟨N⟩. In fact if you take too long typing an abbreviation LocoScript will display the menu anyway, to assist you. Once the menu is displayed like this you must follow the abbreviation with ⟨ENTER⟩. If, however, you quickly type ⟨[+]⟩, ⟨L⟩, ⟨P⟩ and ⟨N⟩ one after the other you do not need to press ⟨ENTER⟩. The only exception is where LocoScript expects a number to follow the code; in these few cases you will need to press ⟨ENTER⟩ after typing the number.

If you make a mistake typing an abbreviation you can correct it using ⟨←DEL⟩. However, you need to be careful as codes themselves can be deleted using this key. Press ⟨[≡]⟩ if you get stuck and need help with the abbreviation.

Don't forget to read the document called READ.ME!

SUMMARY

- A pull-down menu is like a roller blind with a number of options written on it.
- Press ⟨CAN⟩ to abandon an action.
- Press ⟨ENTER⟩ to pass your instructions to LocoScript (to confirm an action).
- Press ⟨EXIT⟩ to quit editing.
- The ⟨RETURN⟩ key is equivalent to the carriage return key on an electric typewriter.
- Use ⟨[+]⟩ to set a paramenter or insert a code. Use ⟨[-]⟩ to clear a setting or to turn off a code.
- Press ⟨STOP⟩ to stop the cursor moving from one part of a document to another.
- The ⟨SHIFT LOCK⟩ key works like that on a typewriter.
- The keyboard uses the standard QWERTY layout but it also has some dedicated word processing keys. In addition to the usual cursor positioning keys it has special textual movement keys.
- The *group* cursor is the upper oblong in the *Disk management* menu.
- The *file* cursor is the lower oblong in the *Disk management menu.*

- *A menu* cursor indicates which option will be selected when you press <ENTER>.
- The *character* cursor is small and flashes.
- The 2nd line of the *Disk management* menu is a sub-menu with 4 options. The 3rd line is a menu with 8 options.
- Whenever you create a new document it adopts its layout characteristics from the TEMPLATE.STD in that group.
- The *ruler line* cursor follows the *character* cursor as you move it left and right.
- The page break shows how many lines have been used and how many remain empty.
- Use the <←DEL> key to delete typing mistakes.
- When you type in text which is longer than the line LocoScript puts in the carriage return automatically.
- When using the *Save and Continue* option of the *Edit options* menu, <UNIT> can be used to return to a UniT code which has previously been placed in the document.
- To display all embedded codes, while editing a document, press <f1> followed by <[+]> and then <ENTER>.
- Use the <RELAY> key to tidy up the display after editing.
- Pressing <ALT> in conjunction with other keys reverses their action.
- <←>, <→>, <↑> and <↓> are cursor control keys.
- <CHAR>, <WORD>, <LINE>, <EOL>, <PARA>, <PAGE> and <DOC> are textual control keys.
- <CHAR> moves the cursor to the next CHARacter.
- <WORD> moves the cursor to the next WORD.
- <EOL> moves the cursor to the End Of the Line.
- <LINE> moves the cursor to the next LINE.
- <PARA> moves the cursor to the end of the PARAgraph.
- <PAGE> moves the cursor to the end of the PAGE.
- <DOC> moves the cursor to the end of the DOCument.
- To delete text press <CUT>, move the cursor and press <CUT> again.
- To copy text press <COPY>, move the cursor and press <COPY> again followed by any number 0 to 9. Move the cursor and press <PASTE> followed by your number.
- To move text press <COPY>, move the cursor and press <CUT> followed by any number 0 to 9. Move the cursor and press <PASTE> followed by your number.
- You can use <FIND> to locate a string of up to 30 characters in your document.
- Use <EXCH> to EXCHange one string of characters with another.
- LocoScript provides five different tabs: (left) Tab (→), Indent Tabs (↦), Right Tab (←), Centre Tab (↔) and Decimal Tab (*).
- Blocks are numbered 0 to 9 and can be saved on disk. Blocks can be whole documents and can be merged with

another document. They are inserted in a document by pressing <PASTE> followed by the number assigned to them.

- LocoScript enables you to store up to 26 short phrases which are labelled A to Z. These phrases can be stored on disk and can be inserted in your documents by pressing <PASTE> followed by the letter assigned to the phrase.
- Changes made to the Base layout are global changes which means they affect the whole document.
- To edit the Base layout from the *Editing text* menu, press <f7>, <ENTER>, <f7> and <f1>.
- With justify on the text will be lined up with the right-hand margin; with justify off the right-hand margin will be ragged.
- LocoScript allows you to vary the pitch between 5 and 17 characters per inch.
- Proportional spacing gives your text a professional look.
- The line pitch can be either 6 or 8 lines per inch.
- The line spacing can be varied between 0 and 3.
- Page length = Header zone + page body + Footer zone.
- LocoScript's *Pagination* menu enables you to control the page layout as well as the page numbering.
- Header and Footer text is independent of the document itself and is not displayed while editing a document.
- LocoScript enables you to have up to 99 different local layouts within a document. Each layout can have up to 99 different tab settings.
- There are different embedded control codes that can be inserted in a document to control its layout and style.
- You can underline sections of text including any spaces or just the words themselves.
- It is possible to cause text to be printed in bold type.
- Using the Double-strike facility when the printer is in its Draft Quality mode produces a different type.
- You can highlight parts of the screen in reverse video.
- LocoScript provides both subscript and superscript characters.
- You can make local changes to the character pitch within a document; when you do this the Base layout pitch is temporarily suspended.
- There are special codes for centring text and for right justifying text.
- You can have hard or soft spaces and/or hyphens.
- The line pitch can be varied locally from within a document.

4 The Printer

The printer can be used in 4 different ways:

(1) to print part or all of a document (that has previously been created/edited and saved on disk) via the P=Print document option of the *Disk management* menu. While the printer is printing one document you can be editing another. If the printer finishes printing before you finish editing then you can start it printing another document by selecting the *Disk management* option of the *Modes* menu. Press <EXIT> to return to editing your document.

(2) to print the whole of a document when you have finished editing it, using the *Save and Print* option of the *Editing text* menu (via the *EXIT* option)

(3) to print line-by-line like an electronic typewriter using the D=Direct printing option of the *Disk management* menu.

(4) to produce an exact copy of what is on the screen (i.e. screen dump).

In addition to the sections called *'Stage 8 Printing'* and *'Appendix II'* in Amstrad's LocoScript Guide (Book 1), there are also sections in their CP/M Guide (Book 1) that refer to the printer. These are *'2.13 Operating the printer'* and *'Appendix II: Advanced use of the printer'*.

Before you attempt to print a document you need to do two things:

(1) get the printer ready for use
(2) tell LocoScript which document to print

If you want to edit one document while another is being printed (this is called background printing) you will find it is quicker to copy the document to be printed into Drive M and have the document that you are editing on Drive A (or Drive B).

4.1 - SETTING UP THE PRINTER

The names of the parts of the printer used here are as shown
in the two diagrams in this chapter.

4.1.1 - Physical location

The printer is connected to the rear of the PCW via a ribbon
cable and an ordinary cable. These cables are rather short and
this restricts where you can position the printer. The only
practical position is to the right of the PCW itself.

If you plan to use continuous stationery then you will
find that the cables get in the way of the paper. One solution
is to raise the printer up on a stand so that the paper is
held clear of the cables. There are a number of purpose-made
stands on the market (see Appendix B).

Another solution is to fit extension cables to allow more
freedom in positioning the printer. While extension cables are
available (see Appendix B) you should try to keep the length to
the minimum necessary otherwise you may experience problems
when using the printer.

4.1.2 - Changing the ribbon cassette

Lift the black dust cover and check that the printer has a
ribbon cassette in it. The dust cover is the rigid plastic
cover with the logo 'Amstrad PCW8256 Printer' on it.

If there isn't a ribbon cassette fitted, then you will
need to fit one. One ribbon cassette is normally supplied with
the PCW. The ribbon cassettes are normally supplied in a box
labelled PT NO Z70216.

Before fitting a ribbon you will need to remove the dust
cover. Note that it may only be removed from the printer by
lifting it while it is in the horizontal position.

Before you insert the ribbon cassette have a look in the
printer and you will see four black projections sticking up;
two at each end. The ribbon cassette clips over these
projections. Also notice the sprocket at the left-hand end that
drives the ribbon.

Now look at the ribbon cassette. Notice the two diagrams
and the 'fin' handle moulded into its top and the rewind knob.

The left-hand diagram shows how to remove the cassette when
it has been fitted to the printer; the right-hand diagram
shows how to locate the ribbon between the mask and the head.
Look at the underside of the cassette and at each end you will
see two little legs with rounded ends (the pair of legs nearest
the rewind knob are quite fragile).

Lower the ribbon cassette gently into the printer while
locating the rewind knob over the sprocket. Press the left-hand
end down first and the right-hand end last. Press it down
firmly to make sure that the legs have clipped over the
projections. Then locate the ribbon itself between the mask and
the print head as shown in the diagram on the cassette top.

Finally take up any slack in the ribbon by turning the
rewind knob clockwise. When removing a cassette hold its fin
and lift the left-hand end first, then gently lift the cassette
clear of the printer. Replace the dust cover when the ribbon
cassette has been fitted.

4.1.3 - Adjusting the print head

The printer will handle ordinary paper; it mustn't be too
flimsy (i.e. less than 50gsm) or too stiff to pass through
properly. The whole point about using a word processor is that
you can print as many NLQ copies as you need whenever you
want to without having to use messy carbon paper. The PCW's
printer cannot be used to prepare spirit masters; if this is
one of your requirements then you will need a daisywheel
printer.

The print head can be adjusted by means of the blue lever
which is located at the inner right-hand end of the printer
(to the right of the ribbon cassette). There are five positions;
if you move the lever back and forth you will see the print
head move with it. Position the lever closest to the platen if
you are using single thin paper; position the lever further
from the platen depending on how many copies you are using.

The normal position for ordinary paper is one click stop from
the end closest to the platen.

4.1.4 - Setting up the printer for single sheet paper

Fit the paper tray extensions to the paper tray. Fit the paper
tray, with its ribbed glossy side towards you, to the printer.

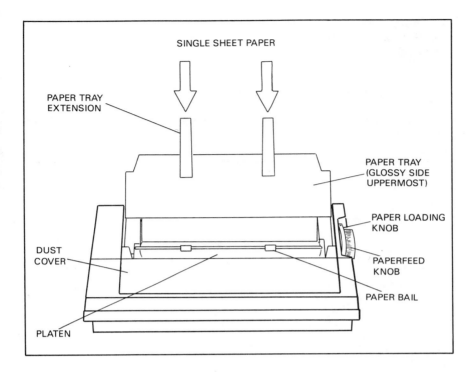

4.1.4.1 - Autoloading the printer

The paper loading and paper feed knobs are located at the right-hand end of the printer. The paper loading knob has a short lever on it; make sure that this is pointing away from you towards the back of the printer.

Now drop a sheet of paper down behind the platen and rest it against the paper tray. Do NOT try to force it under the platen. If you push the paper too far under the platen the printer will detect the presence of the sheet and refuse to load another. Make sure that it is quite near the left-hand end of the platen and then pull the short lever on the paper loading knob towards you. As you pull the lever, the paper bail will move towards you and the paper will be loaded automatically.

Notice that if you have version 1.0 of LocoScript, the print head will move across to the centre and then back to the left-hand side ready for use. However, if you have version 1.2 of LocoScript, then the print head will move to the centre and remain there. It will move back to the left-hand side automatically, the next time the printer is used.

Now, push the short lever towards the back again. If the paper is misaligned, pull the short lever towards you slightly (doing this releases the platen clamp) and realign the paper.

4.1.5 – Setting up the printer for continuous stationery

Fit the paper tray extensions to the paper tray. Fit the paper tray, with its matt side towards you, to the printer.

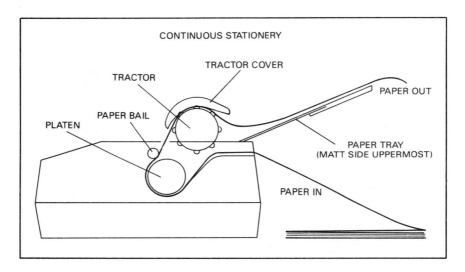

Have a look at the tractor. Underneath you will see a white plastic gear wheel; the tractor should be orientated so that this gear wheel is at the left-hand end. The gear wheel is driven by a similar gear wheel on the platen. Underneath you will also see four projections; two at each end. These projections fit into four slots on the top of the printer. One at each end of the bail bar (when it is positioned away from you) and the other two towards the back of the printer.

Holding the tractor with the gear wheel on the left-hand side but turned away from you (the metal bar should be towards you) locate the two front projections on the tractor in the two slots on the printer at either end of the bail bar. Now lower the back of the tractor and press it down to insert the rear projections in the other two slots.

4.1.5.1 – Continuous stationery

Continuous stationery, which is sometimes called fanfold paper, has the bottom of one page joined to the top of the next. It

normally has perforations down the sides to enable you to
remove the sprocket holes and a perforated page break. Plain
continuous stationery is called listing paper and this is
available with microdot perforations on all four sides of each
sheet which when torn off leaves a clean edge. Continuous
stationery is available in a variety of sizes; while a finished
size of 11"x8½" is common, an A4 equivalent (i.e. 11²/₃"x9¼"
perforated ½" left and right) is freely available (see Appendix
B). Listing paper is normally supplied in boxes of 1000 or
2000 sheets (depending on the weight of paper used; 70gsm is
popular).

Continuous stationery can be single part or multi-part
NCR sets. You can buy continuous stationery that is pre-printed
with your company logo, address, etc. In fact you can buy
continuous stationery pre-printed for all sorts of other jobs
ranging from invoice sets to payroll slips.

You can also get continuous self adhesive computer labels
(one or more across the web) supported on a waxed carrier
sheet. Computer labels are useful for addressing envelopes and
can be obtained pre-printed with your company logo, address,
etc. Labels like this are available (see Appendix B) in various
standard sizes; a common size is 4" by 1¹⁵/₁₆" (web width 5").
They are normally supplied in boxes of 6000 labels.

You will find an example of a standard template for
printing computer labels, called TEMPLATE.LAB, on your working
copy of LocoScript.

The printer is set up for 11 inch continuous stationery
but the settings can easily be changed to enable it to handle
other sizes including A4 and computer labels. You will find
this explained further on in this chapter.

4.1.5.2 - Autoloading the printer

Autoloading the printer with continuous stationery is very
similar to loading single sheet paper. Let the printer feed the
paper in the usual way then move the paper through further
using the paper feed knob until you can engage the paper holes
on the sprockets. Alternatively when the printer has fed the
paper as far as it will go pull the paper loading knob towards
you just enough to release the platen clamp and then pull
through the paper further by hand.

Make sure that the paper feeds through properly by
turning the paper feed knob. Turn it until the line of

perforations is just above the ribbon. The tractor covers
should be down.

Sometimes the paper coming out of the printer tends to be
carried back into the printer by the incoming paper, if this
happens try fitting the paper tray so that its matt side is
towards you. With the tray in this lower position the outgoing
paper is held clear of the incoming paper. A printer stand
helps by allowing the box containing the incoming paper to be
placed under the printer and the outgoing paper to stack itself
behind the printer. You will need to experiment to find the
best setup to suit your particular situation.

4.2 – USING THE PRINTER

You control the printer by putting the PCW into its Printer
Control State. Most other printers have on/off, line feed, form
feed and online/offline switches. The PCW's printer doesn't have
any 'hard' controls like this; all of these functions are
controlled by the software via the keyboard.

Pressing <PTR> (i.e. PrinTeR) puts the PCW into its
Printer Control State enabling you to control the printer. It
is also put into this state automatically when you pull the
paper loading knob towards you, so if you change or adjust the
paper in the printer you are likely to end up with *Printer*
flashing in the top left-hand corner of the screen. This
indicates that the PCW is in its Printer Control State.
Pressing <EXIT> takes the PCW out of its Printer Control State.

Putting the PCW into its Printer Control State stops the
printer. It won't stop immediately; it will stop as soon as it
has finished printing the current line or moving the paper to
the next print position.

If you want to pause the printer press <PTR>; if you want
to continue printing press <EXIT>.

If you want to abandon printing press <PTR> and when the
printer has stopped printing press <f7>, then <ENTER>, finally
press <EXIT>. If you do this you will need to reset the top of
form (see Chapter 4.2.3).

When you press <PTR> the Control zone shows whether the
printer is online (i.e. ready to print) or offline (on standby).
It also shows whether the printer is in use or idle. Note that
it is possible for LocoScript to display that it is in use when
in fact it is not actually printing; it may be trying to print

though, for example when it is waiting for paper (see Chapter 4.2.2).

The bottom line of the Control zone is a menu with 6 options.

4.2.1 - f1=Options

You should always get into the habit of checking the settings in this pull-down menu before you print a document. Press <PTR> and then <f1> to invoke this menu:

```
        Options_____
      ⇥ High quality          0 ⇤
        Draft quality_____
        Single sheet paper     0
        Continuous stationery___
        Form length:          70
        Gap length:            3
        Paper out defeat       0
```


4.2.1.1 - High quality or Draft quality

The first two options enable you to select between the slower Near Letter Quality (NLQ) print and the faster draft quality print.

In NLQ mode it prints at a rate of about 20cps which means that an A4 sheet takes about 3 minutes to print. In draft quality mode it produces about 90cps and can print an A4 page in about 50 seconds. 20cps is equivalent to about 200 words per minute which is not a bad typing speed, particularly when you consider that while the PCW is printing you can be working on another document. The printer is bi-directional; in NLQ mode it makes a second pass to produce the high quality print.

Use the <↓> and <↑> keys to position the cursor and use <[+]> to set a tick against the option that you want. Press <ENTER> to confirm your choice.

If you accidentally start the printer in NLQ mode when you really wanted it to print in draft quality just stop the printer by pressing <PTR>, change the setting in this menu by pressing <f1>, press <ENTER> and then <EXIT>. It will take a few lines to change over from NLQ to draft quality.

4.2.1.2 - Single sheet paper or Continuous stationery

The next two options are also an either/or choice.

If you select *Single sheet paper* LocoScript will automatically adjust the other settings to suit A4 paper i.e. 70 lines per page, with a gap of 6 lines at the top and 3 lines at the bottom of the page (leaving 61 print lines) and *Paper out Defeat* off. If you are not using A4 paper then you will need to change these settings.

If you select *Continuous stationery* then LocoScript will assume that your paper length is 11 inch and change the other settings accordingly: 66 lines per page and a gap of 5 lines at the perforations (note that this leaves 61 print lines, exactly the same as for single sheet paper). If you are using some other size continuous paper (e.g. A4 equivalent) then you will need to change these settings.

4.2.1.3 - Form length

This is the length of the paper measured in terms of the maximum number of standard lines, where a standard line on computer paper is $^1/_6$th of an inch. The form length of A4 paper is 70 lines, 11 inch paper is 66 lines ($66 \times ^1/_6 = 11$). The maximum form length is 99 line (i.e. 16½ inches).

For single sheet paper it doesn't matter if the form length is larger than the actual paper length provided the page size and margin settings are set correctly (see Chapter 3.3.4.7). So you could use A5 paper without having to change the setting from 70 (i.e. A4).

4.2.1.4 - Gap length

This is the number of blank lines that are left at the bottom of each sheet of paper. Normally with A4 paper the gap length is 3, for 11 inch paper it is 5. You can change this setting if you want to.

4.2.1.5 - Paper out defeat

The printer can sense when the paper has run out; if this happens it automatically stops printing. If you set a tick against this option so that when the end of a sheet of paper is reached it will continue printing, the paper out sensor will have been defeated.

When using single sheet paper you need to set a tick

against this option in order to make full use of the length. You do not need a tick when using continuous stationery.

Don't forget to press <EXIT> to stop *Printer* flashing (to leave the Printer Control State) after using this menu.

4.2.2 - f2=Paper

Pressing <PTR> and then <f2> (i.e <SHIFT>+<f1>) invokes a short menu with two options:

```
        Clear "Waiting for Paper"
      ⇥ ● Cancel                    ⇤
```

If you do this now press <CAN> to cancel the menu and press <EXIT> to leave the Printer Control State. This menu is intended for when you are using continuous stationery in the printer but have forgotten to change the *Options* menu setting from *Single sheet paper* to *Continuous stationery*; in this situation LocoScript will stop after printing the first page.

Initially no reason is given for this rude interruption, but if you press <PTR> LocoScript will display the message *Waiting for paper*! This might seem somewhat strange as the printer clearly has plenty of paper in it. What you have to remember is that computers are brilliant at doing *exactly* what they are told to do; you have told it to behave as it would with a single sheet of paper in it!

When using single sheet paper LocoScript stops after printing a page and waits for you to insert the next sheet (to avoid printing on the platen). Normally, LocoScript continues printing (after inserting the next sheet) as soon as it leaves the Printer Control State. Press <EXIT> to leave the Printer Control State.

You will need to alter the *Options* menu from *Single sheet paper* to *Continuous stationery*, so press <f1>. If you don't alter the settings in this menu but just select <f2> and press <ENTER>, then LocoScript will print another page and stop yet again! When you have altered the *Options* menu press <ENTER> to clear the Waiting for Paper State.

Press <f2> and an extended version of the menu will be displayed:

```
        Clear "Waiting for Paper"
      ⇥ ● Confirm                   ⇤
        Cancel
```

Press <ENTER> to confirm that the paper is ready and press <EXIT> to leave the Printer Control State.

You probably won't need to use this menu very often.

WARNING - It is possible to fool LocoScript into 'thinking' that there is paper in the printer when in fact there is not. If this happens and you instruct it to print then it will print on the platen. You should try to avoid this happening, but if it does happen immediately press <PTR> and wait for the printer to stop, then press <f7> followed by <EXIT>.

4.2.3 - f3=Actions

You will frequently need to use this menu, particularly if you use continuous stationery, as it partly replaces the control buttons found on most other printers. Press <PTR> and then <f3>:

```
        :+: to:
      ⇥ Feed one line        ↤
        Feed to top of form
        Set top of form
        Set left offset
        Offset size:      0
```

4.2.3.1 - Feed one line

Pressing <[+]> causes the printer to feed the paper one line (this key does not autorepeat); pressing it repeatedly causes the paper to be fed through the printer one line at a time. If you are using continuous stationery and want to position the paper to set the top of form, first wind the paper through using the paper feed knob and then use this option to finally increment the paper the last few lines.

Press <CAN> or <ENTER> to clear the menu from the screen and then press <EXIT> to leave the Printer Control State.

4.2.3.2 - Feed to top of form

Use <↓> and <↑> to position the *menu* cursor over this option. Pressing <[+]> will cause the printer to feed one sheet of paper through the printer (its length will be determined by the form length). When using continuous stationery, after the last page of a document has been printed, you will need to wind some paper through to be able to get to the last page; this option enables you to do this automatically without having to use the paper feed knob.

Press <CAN> or <ENTER> to clear the menu from the screen
and then press <EXIT> to leave the Printer Control State.

4.2.3.3 - Set top of form

This option enables you to tell LocoScript, when using
continuous stationery, where you want the page to begin. Use
<↓> and <↑> to move the *menu* cursor to this option, position
the paper as you want it and press <[+]>.

Press <CAN> or <ENTER> to clear the menu from the screen
and then press <EXIT> to leave the Printer Control State.

4.2.3.4 - Set left offset
Offset size:

This option enables the print head to be offset from the left-
hand end of the platen. To use this feature position the *menu*
cursor over *Offset size:* and type a number between 0 and 69
followed by <ENTER>. The print head will immediately move to
that position and all subsequent printing will be offset from
the left-hand end of the platen by that amount. Press <CAN> or
<ENTER> to clear the menu from the screen and then press
<EXIT> to leave the Printer Control State.

This feature can be used to position screen dumps
laterally; unless you use this feature screendumps are printed
at the left-hand end of the platen. It is also useful for
positioning addresses on computer labels and when Direct
printing (see Chapter 4.4).

You could use this feature to print separate columns on
one page. Store the different columns in different pages. Print
one page, move the paper back and use the *Print some pages*
menu to print the next column, and so on. While this would be
rather tedious it might be worth considering.

4.2.4 - Note that there is no f4 option in this menu.

4.2.5 - f5=Document/Reprint

If you press <PTR> and then <f5> a menu like this will be
displayed:

```
        Not printing a document
      ⇥ 0 Cancel                    ⇤
```

However, if you press <PTR> and then <f5> while printing
a document the printer will stop (because you have pressed
<PTR>) and a menu similar to this will be displayed:

```
Name: REPRINT#.DOC
   From page      1
   This page      7
   To page       12
⇥ Reprint            ⇤
   This page
   From beginning
```

One purpose of this menu is to give you details of the
document that is being printed. For example this document is
called REPRINT#.DOC, it is 12 pages long and the printer was
stopped while page 7 was being printed. When you are ready to
continue printing press <CAN> or <ENTER> to clear the menu
from the screen, then press <EXIT> to resume printing. The
other purpose of this menu is to enable you to reprint pages
if the paper gets jammed in the printer for some reason. First
clear the mangled paper from the printer and get the paper
passing freely again using the paper feed knob, then press <↓>
and the menu will extend like this:

```
Name: REPRINT#.DOC
   From page      1
   This page      7
   To page       12
   Reprint
⇥ 0 This page        ⇤
   From beginning
   Reposition paper at Top
   of Form before allowing
   printing to continue
```

If you now press <ENTER> and then <EXIT> LocoScript will
resume printing from page 7. However, if you move the *menu*
cursor down to the *From beginning* option LocoScript will
reprint the whole document from page 1 to page 12. You
probably won't use this menu very often; if you want to see
how many pages there are in a document you can do this
without having to print it (see Chapter 4.3).

4.2.6 – Note that there is no f6 option in this menu.

4.2.7 - f7=Reset

You will have to use this option whenever you need to abandon
printing. Press <PTR> and then <f7> to invoke the menu; press
<ENTER> to abandon printing. Press <EXIT> to leave the Printer
Control State.

```
        Abandon printing and reset
     ⇥ ● Confirm                      ⇤
        Cancel
```

Note that after pressing <f7> you will need to reset the
top of form.

4.2.8 - f8=On/Off Line

Pressing <f8> (i.e. <SHIFT>+<f7>) alternately puts the printer
online or offline (to the PCW). The printer must be online for
the PCW to be able to print a document. Sometimes it is useful
to be able to take the printer offline while you get on with
another job; you will need to put it back online to finish
printing.

For example, suppose you are editing a document called
ALPHA and want to print another document called OMEGA without
quitting ALPHA. Press <f7> to invoke the *Modes* menu and move
the *menu* cursor to the *Disc management* option and press
<ENTER>. Locoscript will temporarily leave ALPHA and display
Disc management whilst editing (you can return to ALPHA at any
time by pressing <EXIT>). Now move the *file* cursor to OMEGA
and press <P> followed by <ENTER>. The printer will start
printing OMEGA and you can return to editing ALPHA by pressing
<EXIT>.

Imagine that a friend arrives and you want to demonstrate
using LocoScript to edit ALPHA but you don't want to have the
noise of OMEGA printing in the background. Press <PTR> to
invoke the Printer Control State and to stop OMEGA printing.
Press <f8> to put the printer offline, press <EXIT> to quit
from the Printer Control State and press <EXIT> again to
resume editing ALPHA.

When your friend has gone and you want to resume
printing OMEGA press <PTR>, <f8> and <EXIT> twice. Now you can
get on with the job of editing ALPHA again. If you wanted to
you could finish editing ALPHA and save it on disk while OMEGA
is still printing, and start editing another document.

Note that the combined process of editing ALPHA at the same time as printing OMEGA will take a little longer if both documents are on Drive A. It would speed up the process if you copied OMEGA from Drive A to Drive M before you started printing it. This can be done while still editing ALPHA by selecting the *Disc management* option as before.

4.3 - P=Print document (*Disk management* MENU OPTION)
TELLING LOCOSCRIPT WHICH DOCUMENT TO PRINT

Position the *group* cursor over the group which contains the document that you want to print, then position the *file* cursor over the name of the document to be printed. Press <P> and a pull-down menu will be displayed. If you are using LocoScript version 1.0, then a pull-down menu similar to this will be displayed:

<u>Print document</u>
→ Name: DOCUMENT.000 ←
  Group: LETTERS
  Drive: A

Note that version 1.0 does not allow you to print individual pages. When you are ready to print the document just press <ENTER>.

If you want to pause the printer, at any time, press <PTR>; press <EXIT> to resume printing. If you want to abandon printing altogether, press <PTR> to stop printing, press <f7> to reset the printer, finally press <EXIT> to stop *Printer* from flashing in the Control zone.

If you are using LocoScript version 1.2 then the menu will look similar to this:

<u>Print document</u>
→ Name: DOCUMENT.000 ←
  Group: LETTERS
  <u>Drive: A</u>
⊕ Print all pages
  Print some pages

Notice LocoScript assumes that you want to print all pages, hence there is a tick against *Print all pages*. If you want to select this option then just press <ENTER>.

If you only want to print some pages, then move the *menu* cursor down, to the *Print some pages* option using <↓>, before

you press <ENTER>. Note that the tick moves with the *menu*
cursor. When you press <ENTER> another menu will be displayed.
For example:

    Print some pages
    Name: DOCUMENT.000
    First page: 1
    ⇥ From page: 1   ⇤
    To page: 10
    Last page: 10

Imagine that you want to print only page 7. Press <7>
then press <ENTER>, to get LocoScript to accept the change.
Press <↓> to move the *menu* cursor down to the *To page* option.
Press <7> again, and then press the <ENTER> key again to get
LocoScript to accept the change. Finally press <ENTER> once
more to tell LocoScript to start printing the page.

So to recap press: <7> <ENTER> <↓> <7> <ENTER> <ENTER>

If you want to see how many pages there are in a
document all you need to do is invoke the menu in this way,
check the last page number and then press <CAN> to clear the
menu from the screen.

If you attempt to use the printer while it is actually
printing a document (or while LocoScript *thinks* it is printing
a document) then the following error message will be displayed
on the screen:

    Error in: Print document
    The printer is active
    ⇥ ⊗ Printer now idle: retry ⇤
    Cancel operation

When this happens LocoScript is trying to tell you that
the printer is already in use (or active). The word *Printing* is
always displayed in the Control zone whenever LocoScript is
using the printer (or trying to use it). The menu option that
you are being offered (it has a tick alongside it) is not a lot
of use to you if LocoScript is using the printer. In fact if
you try to accept this option by pressing <ENTER> the error
message will be repeated.

If the printer is actually printing something that you
want, then you will have to:

        either wait for it to finish printing the first
        document and then press <ENTER> to start printing
        the second document

or press ⟨↓⟩ followed by ⟨ENTER⟩ to cancel the
request to print the second document

If you want to stop the first document from being printed
while this error message is displayed, press ⟨PTR⟩ to stop the
printer, then press ⟨f7⟩ to reset the printer and finally press
⟨EXIT⟩ to stop *Printer* flashing in the Control zone.

When you finally press ⟨EXIT⟩ this will cause the error
message to be displayed again inviting you to *retry*. If you
still want to print the second document, you will first need to
reset the top of form setting, because by pressing ⟨f7⟩ you
will have reset the printer so that LocoScript now assumes the
current position to be the correct top of form setting. So you
need to press ⟨↓⟩ followed by ⟨ENTER⟩ to select the *Cancel
operation* option, set the top of form and then print the second
document.

If you attempt to print a document which LocoScript is
already trying to print, the following error message will be
displayed:

> Error in: Print document
> File is already in use
> ⇥ ● Cancel operation   ⇤

This time you are not given an alternative; just press
⟨ENTER⟩ to *Cancel operation*!

4.4 – D=Direct printing ⟨*Disk management* MENU⟩

Pressing ⟨D⟩ invokes a pull-down menu like this:

> ⇥ ● confirm ⇤
> cancel

By displaying this pull-down menu LocoScript is inviting
you to confirm that you want the *Direct printing* mode. Notice
the tick against *confirm*. If you press ⟨↓⟩ then the tick moves
down to *cancel*; pressing ⟨↑⟩ moves it back up. If you don't
want the *Direct printing* mode, simply move the tick and press
⟨ENTER⟩. If you do this, you will be returned to the original
Disk management menu. To try out the *Direct printing* mode
press ⟨D⟩ and then ⟨ENTER⟩, when the tick is against *confirm*.

When you enter the *Direct printing* mode the screen
display changes. Try typing in a few words but don't press
⟨RETURN⟩, yet.

When you press <RETURN> the printer will print out what you have typed in. The screen will also clear, ready for you to enter more text. Your text isn't printed until you press <RETURN>. You can make your text longer than one line; you just have to resist the temptation to press <RETURN>!

The *Direct printing* mode can be very useful as you can use any of LocoScript's word processing functions; for example, you can use it for addressing envelopes or filling in forms. LocoScript's basic word processing facilities are described more fully in Chapter 3.2.

To quit the *Direct printing* mode press <EXIT>. Pressing <EXIT> from *Direct printing* mode invokes another pull-down menu. This time the options are:

> → 0 Finish direct printing ←
> Abandon direct printing

Notice that there is a tick against the first option so that if you press <ENTER> you are returned to the *Disk management* menu. If you have typed in something which hasn't been printed yet and select *Finish direct printing*, then what you have typed in will be printed when you press the <ENTER> key. If you press <↓>, followed by <ENTER>, then the text entered since you last pressed <RETURN> will be lost.

4.5 - MAKING SCREENDUMPS

If you press <EXTRA> followed by <PTR> the PCW will produce what is called a screendump. This is literally a line by line copy of everything on the screen.

Use the *Actions* menu to offset the screendump and position it in the centre of the paper. You can produce a screendump from anywhere in LocoScript; you can also use this feature when running other programs under CP/M. For example you can use it to produce hardcopy printouts of your LOGO designs.

SUMMARY

- The printer can be used to print copies of your documents, as a line by line printer or to produce screendumps.
- The printer loads its paper automatically.
- It can be used with either single sheet paper or continuous stationery.

- Press <PTR> to enter the Printer Control State, or to stop the printer if it is printing.
- Press <EXIT> to leave the Printer Control State, or to continue printing if the printer is printing.
- You should always check the f1=Options menu before using the printer.
- You can print selected pages of a document.
- Use the f3=Actions menu to position the paper and set top of form when using continuous stationery.
- To feed continuous stationery forward one sheet after printing press <PTR>, <f3>, <↓>, <[+]>, <ENTER> and then <EXIT>!
- Press <EXTRA>+<PTR> to produce a screendump.

5 Other Features

The PCW was designed for Amstrad by the design consultancy MEJ Electronics near Guildford, England and is manufactured in Korea.

5.1 - HARDWARE

Generally speaking, hardware comprises those bits of equipment that you can touch.

The machine is called the PCW because it is a Personal Computer configured as a Word processor. It is called the 8256 or 8512 because it is based on an 8-bit microprocessor chip and has 256K or 512K bytes of RAM.

A bit is a binary digit, i.e. either 0 or 1. Microprocessors are programmed in a low-level programming language called machine code which comprises instructions in a binary coded form. A group of 8 bits is called a byte. The memory in the computer is subdivided into locations, each comprising one byte (or 8 bits) of data (e.g. 11001100). The largest number that can be stored by one byte is 2^8 (256). A group of 256 memory locations is called a page of memory.

1K of memory is 2^{10} (1024) bytes, or four pages of memory ($4\times256=1024$ bytes). N.B. The K used in computing should not be confused with k (kilo) which in the International System of units (SI) is used to represent 1000. An 8-bit microprocessor can address a maximum of 256 pages of memory directly ($256\times256=65536$ bytes), which is 64K bytes of memory ($65536\div1024=64K$ bytes). Although the PCW's Z80 microprocessor chip can only address 64K bytes of RAM, the PCW makes use of its 256K (or 512K) bytes of RAM by employing a technique called bank-switching. The operating system software switches one bank of RAM out and another into view.

RAM (*R*andom *A*ccess *M*emory) is the computer's memory, so 256K of RAM is the size of the computer's memory. Sometimes RAM is called volatile memory because when you switch the power off its contents (documents/data/programs) are destroyed. Some computers also use another kind of memory called ROM (*R*ead *O*nly *M*emory); this is non-volatile and is used to store programs permanently.

The PCW contains no discrete ROM (Read Only Memory) chips; the machine code program called the bootstrap, needed to load CP/M Plus (or LocoScript) into RAM from disk, is held in the 256 bytes of masked ROM available in the 8041 printer controller chip (see Chapter 5.2.1).

5.1.1 - Monitor

While most other business systems provide an 80 column by 25 line display, the PCW has 90 columns by 32 lines, which provides 44% more characters on the screen than usual. This larger size can be useful when using word processor or spreadsheet programs like Supercalc 2 which have been configured to take advantage of this feature. Digital Research's GSX graphics interface software which is supplied can display graphics at a resolution of 720×256 pixels. Computers make pictures by lighting up tiny squares on the screen called pixels. The word pixel is derived from *picture element*.

5.1.2 - CPS8256
Centronics Parallel/RS232C Serial Interface

At the rear of the VDU there is an expansion edge connector which leads from the main PCB. An interface module called the CPS8256 is available which plugs into this edge connector; it slots into a recess on the back panel and derives its power from inside the PCW.

The CPS8256 has a serial interface which is intended for use in conjunction with serial interface printers, plotters, etc. and to provide a connection to modems and the serial ports of other computers.

For example, given a CPS8256 and modem you can use your PCW and a standard telephone line for sending and receiving TELEX messages as well as all types of electronic mail. You can also use it to access PRESTEL and other Viewdata systems. A single serial input/output connector is provided which conforms to the industry standard pinout and RS232C voltage requirements for a terminal.

The CPS8256 also has a parallel 'Centronics' interface which is intended for use with parallel interface printers, plotters, etc. An industrial standard 36 way connector is used. The length of cable that you can use will depend on your printer but you should get satisfactory results with up to 2 metres of cable.

It is possible to use both the serial interface and the parallel port simultaneously. For example, you could have your alternative printer connected to the parallel port and a modem connected to the serial interface.

Software that allows the PCW to address the CPS8256's serial interface and parallel port as standard peripherals is included in the bundled software. This facilitates computer input and allows output to be directed to the CPS8256 instead of the PCW's screen or printer.

A simple Mail Terminal Program is bundled with the PCW which allows you to access dial-up databases, information services, etc. as well as providing facilities for emulating a standard terminal when connecting the PCW to a minicomputer as a VDU.

A comprehensive manual that describes the connections required, the **CP/M Plus** facilities available, as well providing instructions for the Mail Terminal Program, is supplied with the CPS8256.

If you want to use the CPS8256 with another printer you will probably have to buy another word processor as well (see Appendix A).

5.1.3 - Printer

The PCW's 80 column dot matrix printer is made by Seikosha; it takes its power from the 24V connector on the back of the VDU. Usually, printers contain a microprocessor of their own, a ROM to store various character fonts, as well as electronics for a printer interface and on/off, online/offline, line-feed and form-feed controls. The PCW's printer has none of these as all of these functions are controlled via the software and using the keyboard. Its interface is non-standard; if you want to drive another printer you will need to use the CPCS256 interface.

While **LocoScript** allows you to produce documents that are wider than the screen, if you want to print a document that is more than 80 columns wide then you will have to use another printer. If you choose to use another printer remember that **LocoScript** uses special embedded control codes to drive the PCW's printer. These codes will not be recognised by another printer and will have to be removed from your document file. Use the ASCII file option within **LocoScript** version 1.2 to create a version of your document which doesn't have these codes (see Chapter 2.7.1.7). Alternatively use another word processor (see Appendix A).

It is possible to print graphics, either by using the screen dump routine provided or by using Digital Research's Graphics System Extension (**GSX**) to **CP/M Plus**. This is additional system software which converts graphics instructions produced by a **CP/M Plus** program into instructions which can be understood by the printer.

5.2 - SOFTWARE

Programs for a computer are called the software. There are two main types of software:

system software
applications software

5.2.1 - System software

The system software is needed by the computer itself in order to enable it to operate as intended by the manufacturer. An operating system is a special program that controls the system's resources and demands placed on those resources. It is the operating system that gives a microcomputer many of its characteristics.

CP/M (Control Program for Microcomputers) is a disk-based operating system, which means that before the computer can be used the operating system must first be loaded into RAM from a disk. A special program called a bootstrap is used to do this and is invoked by pressing <SHIFT>, <EXTRA> and <EXIT> all at the same time. The bootstrap is also used to load LocoScript when it is present on the disk. The term is reputed to originate from a story told by Baron Munchausen who boasted that finding himself trapped and sinking in a swamp, he lifted himself by his bootstraps and carried himself to safety on firm ground.

The PCW's main operating system is Digital Research's **CP/M Plus** (Version 3.0 or 3.0 Banked, as it is also called). There have been various versions of CP/M since it was first developed in 1975: 1.3, 1.4, 2.0, 2.2, 3.0 and Plus, so you need to take care when buying CP/M software that it is fully compatible with the PCW.

If you have used CP/M before then you will be interested to learn **CP/M Plus** was developed specifically for the range of Z80 8-bit machines, like the PCW, which use more than 64K of RAM, enabling RAM to be bank-switched. **CP/M Plus** is more user friendly and more powerful than the earlier CP/M Version 2.2 and includes many improvements. For example, the old BDOS ERROR ON A has been replaced with the more friendly invitation to Retry, Abort or Ignore, and there is now an on-screen help facility which can be loaded to explain how the various CP/M commands work. Other enhancements include date stamping of files, password protection and a more powerful version of the DIR command.

CP/M Plus on the PCW8256 doesn't give you access to all 256K of RAM. 116K is set aside as a RAM disk; so far as the operating system is concerned this is treated as a very fast disk and designated drive M. 79K is used by **CP/M Plus**, leaving 61K for the transient program area (TPA); this is used to store your application program. At first sight, it might seem that 61K out of 256K isn't very good, but in fact it is more than enough to run most of the popular CP/M applications programs.

If you have used CP/M before then you should know that the 79K of RAM grabbed by **CP/M Plus** is divided between the basic input/output system (BIOS), the basic disk operating system (BDOS), the console command processor (CCP) and the disk hash tables. If you are new to CP/M then all you really need to know is that having BIOS, BDOS, and CCP in RAM is useful because it means that you have only to load the disk once.

CP/M Plus is set up on the PCW so that even if you have only one physical drive, it can be designated Drive A or Drive B; you can pretend to be copying from Drive A to Drive B. The system automatically tells you when to swap disks. The name of the current virtual drive is displayed in the bottom right-hand corner of the screen.

Because **CP/M Plus** needs to be loaded into RAM once only it isn't required to be present on subsequent disks; that is, provided that it isn't replaced by loading **LocoScript**. Loading **LocoScript** replaces **CP/M Plus** in RAM and vice versa. **LocoScript** embodies its own operating system and, when it is used, doesn't require **CP/M Plus**.

The right-hand end of the keyboard houses a numeric keypad which can be used either with **CP/M Plus** or with **LocoScript** (see Appendix C). If you are used to using **CP/M Plus** then you will find the *ConTroL key* is labelled <ALT> and the *ESCape key* is labelled <EXIT>; you will probably need to use these keys if you decide to run other CP/M software.

Under **CP/M Plus** the PCW's keyboard can be set up to one of eight character sets: American, French, German, English, Danish, Swedish, Italian, or Spanish.

5.2.2 - Applications software

These are the programs that you need to suit your particular application. When you want to use the PCW specifically as a WP then you use the application program called **LocoScript**. **CP/M Plus** enables you to use all kinds of other applications software such as spreadsheet programs, database programs, etc. There is a lot of CP/M software already available for the PCW; the range is still growing (see Appendix A)!

5.2.2.1 - LocoScript

LocoScript was written by a software house called Locomotive Software, hence the name. Unlike other WPs, such as **VordStar**, **LocoScript** has been written specifically for the PCW and therefore can take full advantage of its particular hardware configuration. **LocoScript** uses CP/M file structures; data is available to **CP/M Plus** and vice versa.

5.2.2.2 - LOGO

DR LOGO is a programming language that is often used in schools. The DR stands for Digital Research, the publishers of both **DR LOGO** and **CP/M Plus** itself. Like the programming language called BASIC, there are lots of different versions or dialects of LOGO. While LOGO was designed to be used by children you don't have to be a child to be able derive a bit of fun from it!

To be able to use **DR LOGO** you will first have to rename a file on your copy of **CP/M Plus**, from PROFILE.ENG to PROFILE.SUB. To do this load **CP/M Plus** into the PCW by resetting the PCW with the **CP/M Plus** disk in the drive, then type DIR and press <RETURN> to list all the files on the disk. You should be able to see PROFILE.ENG. Next type RENAME PROFILE.SUB=PROFILE.ENG and press <RETURN> and then reset the PCW again. This time it will load a series of files including

SETKEYS.COM into Drive M (if you don't have SETKEYS.COM in
Drive M then **DR LOGO** will crash when you press <EXIT> to
abandon an edit).

Now you can remove the **CP/M Plus** disk and insert your
copy of **DR LOGO**. Type LOGO followed by <RETURN> (not SUBMIT
LOGO as Amstrad's Book 1 suggests). Don't forget to use the
PCW's screen dump facility to produce hardcopy printouts of
your masterpieces! When you want to return to the CP/M prompt
type BYE, followed by <RETURN>.

If you want to learn more about **DR LOGO**, Amsoft produce a
book which is available from the Amstrad Users Group (see
Appendix B); you will find that there are other books
available. For example, Macmillan publish a book called
Microchild, Learning through LOGO by Serafim Gascoigne; ISBN
0-333-37450-9.

5.2.2.3 - BASIC

BASIC is a popular programming language; if you haven't already
used BASIC then you should try to use it, as programming can
be fun and is not just for the experts. Amstrad supply
Locomotive Software's **Mallard BASIC** 'free' with the PCW.
Mallard BASIC is no mean BASIC; in fact with its **JETSAM**
extensions it is a very powerful version of the language.
JETSAM is a file manager or index sequential access manager
(ISAM) which turns **Mallard BASIC** into something like a
database authoring system. Its main strength arises out of its
file handling capabilities. However, if you're interested in
converting **BBC BASIC** programs then you may be disappointed;
there are no graphics facilities at all.

Before you can use **Mallard BASIC** you will have to load
CP/M Plus into the PCW, then type BASIC followed by <RETURN>.
When you want to leave **Mallard BASIC** type SYSTEM followed by
<RETURN>.

If you want graphics then you might like to consider
using Digital Research's **C-BASIC**. Their version includes
graphics but runs more slowly than **Mallard BASIC**, despite
being a compiled version of the language!

5.2.2.4 - Other CP/M software

Installing other CP/M applications programs on the PCW has
been made as simple as possible. In order to avoid conversion
problems the PCW employs special emulation software which
convinces your application program that it is dealing with a

standard DEC VT52 terminal instead of the PCW. As most CP/M applications software can be configured to work with a DEC terminal, the potential problem of incompatibility never arises because your application program doesn't see a PCW.

The same thing has been done with the printer. Instead of your application program dealing with the printer directly, it is tricked by an Epson emulator; it can then be configured as though it were working with an Epson dot matrix printer.

Next to word processing, microcomputers like the PCW are probably most commonly used for processing data. Spreadsheets are very popular with accountants because you can play the 'what if' game; what happens if my income increases by 10%, what if our overheads increase by 4%? Of course, the other popular application is the processing of records to produce a database.

You can get all sorts of other programs to run on your PCW, including complete accounting packages, programming languages like BASIC, C, COBOL, FORTRAN, PASCAL as well as programming tools like cross assemblers. You can also get alternative word processors, communications software, project planners, computer aided learning packages and some recreational games.

Word processors can even be used for editing computer programs. Some word processors like **WordStar** and **NewWord** have non-document modes allowing BASIC programs to be edited. In fact **NewWord** has a *Run a Program* option that allows BASIC programs to be run from within the word processor.

If you run a small business, software packages like **Cash Trader** are available to help do your accounting for you; it automatically accumulates VAT and a printed report is available for VAT and audit purposes. You can create your own entry and analysis heads: these can be created even in the middle of an entry, giving total flexibility in the analysis of income and expenditure. **Cash Trader** includes a number of examples and training exercises so that you can become thoroughly familiar with it before entrusting your company's valuable data to it!

One particular program has created a brand new category of its own; you can use **Brainstorm** as a thought processor. It internally relates and structures ideas, putting them back to you in a structured way. Its applications are really only limited by your imagination; it's like a word processor, spreadsheet and database all rolled into one!

Much of the software that has been made available for the PCW is priced under £50; often there is no difference (apart from the price) between a package for the PCW and its counterpart for machines like the IBM PC, which cost many times more. Because the PCW has been sold in such large numbers software houses are taking advantage of this growing market; from their point of view the PCW has rejuvenated the CP/M market, so make sure that you take advantage of these lower costs. A good example of low cost software for the PCW is the highly acclaimed **Mini Office II**; don't be fooled by its low cost.

Macmillan publish a useful book called *Understanding Management Software* by Andrew Leigh (ISBN 0-333-40946-9) that critically reviews 30 popular software packages many of which can be run on the PCW; it includes a Guide to Computer Training Agencies. If you use your PCW in a business environment then you will find Macmillan's *The Computer Handbook, A Businessman's Guide to Choosing and Using a Computer System* by Charles Jones (ISBN 0-333-39263-9) invaluable; it is crammed full with all kinds of useful information.

Remember, your PCW is *more* than just a word processor!

SUMMARY

- PCW8256 = Personal Computer Word Processor which uses the 8 bit Z80 microprocessor chip and has 256K bytes of memory (the PCW8512 has 512K bytes of memory).
- 1K byte = 4 pages = 1024 bytes.
- 1 page = 256 bytes.
- 1 byte = 8 bits.
- A bit is a *binary digit*, i.e. 0 or 1.
- RAM = Random Access Memory; contents are lost when PCW is switched off.
- The PCW uses a 14-inch screen, 90 columns across by 32 lines down with a resolution of 720×256 pixels.
- CP/M Plus uses the bank-switching technique to enable the Z80 microprocessor to access 256K (or 512K) bytes.
- The optional CPS8256 interface allows a faster printer to be used or communications via modem.
- System and applications programs are collectively called software.
- System software enables the computer to control the hardware. It determines the applications software that can be used.

- The PCW uses the CP/M Plus operating system except when it is using LocoScript.
- When using CP/M Plus <ALT> = Control and <EXIT> = Escape.
- CP/M Plus sets aside 116K as RAM disk, 79K for its own use, 61K for your application program.
- Applications software enables the computer to do a particular job e.g. word processing.
- DR LOGO and Mallard BASIC are programming languages.

Appendix A   CP/M Software

A major feature of the PCW8256/8512 is that it uses the CP/M operating system which means you can use a wide range of standard software products. Note that some of this software requires a second disk drive.

Because new software is continually being made available for these machines it is impossible to produce a complete list. However, it is hoped that this list (compiled in Summer 1986) will demonstrate that the PCW is more than just a Word Processor!

TITLE	FROM	TYPE
ABC Suite	Quest	Sales Invoicing
		Sales Ledger
		Stock Control
		Purchase Ledger
		Nominal Ledger
A.B.C.S.	Amsoft	Sales/Debtors Ledger
		Sales Invoicing
		System
		Stock Control System
		Purchase/Creditors
		Ledger
		Nominal/General
		Ledger
Amstrad Paymaster	Amsoft	Payroll system
Analyser	Quest	Report generator
		(see Cash Trader)
Assembler Plus	MicroSoft	Programming tool
Aztec C II	Manx	Programming tool
Back-up	Xitan	Copy utility
BASIC	Nevada	Programming language
BASIC Compiler	MicroSoft	Programming language
Brainstorm	Caxton	Ideas processor
		3-D scratchpad
CBASIC Compiler	Digital Research	Programming language
		compiler

C	BDS	Programming language compiler
C	HiSoft	Programming language compiler
CalcStar	MicroPro	Spreadsheet
Camsoft Business Software	Camsoft	Database Nominal Ledger Payroll Purchase Ledger Sales Invoicing Sales Ledger Stock Control
Cardbox Cardbox Plus	Caxton	Database
Cash Trader	Quest	Accounting package (see Analyser)
Catalog	HiSoft	Disk organiser
Chit-Chat	SageSoft	Communications
CIS-COBOL	MicroFocus	Programming language
Classic Adventure	Abersoft	Text adventure game
COBOL	Microsoft	Programming language
Compact Accounts Compact Daybook	Compact Software	Accounting packages
DataGem	Gemini	Database
DataStar	MicroPro	Database
dBaseII	Ashton-Tate	Database
Delta 1.25	Comsoft	Database
Devpac80	HiSoft	Programming tool
DR Draw DR Graph	Digital Research	Graphics utilities
DR LOGO	Digital Research	Programming language (supplied with PCW)
ECO-C	EcoSoft	Programming language
ED80	HiSoft	Programming tool
File Expander	Quest	File utility (see ABC Suite)
Flexifile	Saxon	Database
FORTRAN	MicroSoft	Programming language
FORTRAN	Nevada	Programming language
FORTRAN	Prospero	Programming language
GEN80	HiSoft	Programming tool
Hands-On CP/M	MicroCal	CP/M training
Hands-On COBOL	MicroCal	COBOL training
Hands-On DBaseII	MicroCal	DBaseII training
Hands-On Multiplan	MicroCal	Multiplan training
HoneyComm HoneyTerm HoneyView	HoneySoft	Communications utilities
Invoice Spooler	Quest	Invoicing utility

LocoScript	Locomotive Soft	Word processor (supplied with PCW)
Macro 80	Microsoft	Programming tool
Mallard BASIC	Locomotive Soft	Programming language (supplied with PCW)
MasterPlanner	Comshare	Financial modeller
MatchBox	Quest	Electronic card index system
MailMerge	MicroPro	Mailmerge option for WordStar
MicroProlog	LPA	Programming language
Mini Office II	Database Software	Word processor, Database, Spreadsheet, Graphics, Communications Label Printer
Modula-2	HiSoft	Programming language
Mordon's Quest	Abersoft	Text Adventure Game
Multiplan	Microsoft	Spreadsheet for financial planning
NewWord	NewStar	Word processor (see The WordPlus)
PASCAL/MT+	Digital research	Programming language
PASCAL80	HiSoft	Programming language
PASCAL	Prospero	Programming language
PC Soft Modules	Datasoftware Intl	Invoicing Sales Ledger Stockledger Purchase Ledger Nominal Ledger
Pertmaster	Abtex	Critical path analysis
PILOT	Nevada	Programming language
PlannerCalc	Sorcim	Financial modeller
PlannerCalc2		
Pocket CalcStar	MicroPro	Spreadsheet
Pocket DataStar	MicroPro	Database
Pocket ReportStar	MicroPro	Report generator
Pocket WordStar	MicroPro	Word processor
Polyplot	Arcom Software	Histograms, pie charts and graphs
Polyprint	Arcom	Font aid
Polymail	Arcom	Mail merge
Polyword	Arcom	Word processor
ReportStar	MicroPro	Report generator
Sage Popular Accounts	SageSoft	Sales/Purchase Ledger Reports Nominal Ledger

		Invoicing
		Payroll
Sage Retrieve	SageSoft	Database
ScratchPad Plus	Caxton	Spreadsheet
		virtual memory
ShoeBox	Quest	Accounting utility
		links to WordStar
Sort	Microsoft	Sort utility
SpellStar	MicroPro	Spelling checker
		option for WordStar
StarCom	NewStar	Communications
		utility
Supercalc	Sorcim	Spreadsheets aid
Supercalc2		financial planning
SuperSort	MicroPro	Sort utility
Smart Key	Caxton	Utilities
Smart Key II		
Target Task	via NewStar	Project planner
The Accounting	via NewStar	Database
Solution		
The Cracker	Software Tech	Spreadsheet with
The Cracker2	(Ian Searle)	graphics
The Hitchhikers	Infocom	Text adventure game
Guide to the		
Galaxy		
The Knife	HiSoft	Disk sector editor
The Torch	HiSoft	CP/M training
The WordPlus	Oasis Systems	Spelling checker
		(links to NewWord)
Time Recorder	Quest	Time and cost
		recorder
Touch 'N' Go	Caxton	Training
Two Fingers	Iansyst	Typing retraining
Typing Crash Course	Iansyst	Typing training
Turbo PASCAL	Borland	Programming language
Wordlink	Quest	Links ABC Suite to
		WordStar
WordStar	MicroPro	Word processor
WP workshop (W/S)	MAC	WordStar training
WP workshop (M/M)	MAC	MailMerge training
Write Hand Man	Poor Person Soft	CP/M utility
XASM04 (6804)	Avocet	Cross assembler
XASM05 (6805)		programming tools
XASM09 (6809)		
XASM18 (1802/05)		
XASM48 (8048/41)		
XASM51 (8051)		
XASM65 (6502)		
XASM68 (6800/01)		

```
XASMF8(F8/3870)
XASMZ8(Z8)
XASMZ80(Z80)
XASM85(8085/Z80)
XASM400(COP400)
XASM75(NEC7500)
XMAC68K(68000)
XBASIC              Xitan            Programming language
ZBASIC              Zedcor           Programming language
```

Appendix B   Useful Addresses

You should find these addresses and notes useful. However, this
is not intended to be a comprehensive list of all suppliers of
hardware or software for the PCW. While this information was
checked carefully when it was compiled (Summer 1986) you might
find that the address you want has changed. If you have
difficulty check the advertisements in a magazine like *'Amstrad
Computer User'*.

ADDRESS

NOTE

Advanced Memory Systems Ltd
Warrington
WA4 1BR
Tel: 0925 413501

Producers of the AMX Mouse
and AMX Pagemaker.

Amstrad Consumer
Electronics plc
Brentwood House
169 King's Road
Brentwood
Essex
CM14 4EF
Tel: 0277 228888
Customer Services
Tel: 0277 230222

Amstrad Computer User
169 Kings Road
Brentwood
Essex
CM14 4EF
Tel: 0277-234434

This is the official Amstrad
magazine which you get 'free'
if you are a member of the
'Amstrad User Club'; it is
included in the subscription.
It also contains a supplement
called *'Amstrad Business
Computing'*.

Amstrad User Club
AMSOFT
Victoria House
P O Box 10
Sunderland
SR13PY
Tel: 0783 673395

Annual subscription includes
12 issues of *'Amstrad Computer
User'*, Amsoft Software
Catalogue, worth joining for
the 15% discount.
For example: ribbons,
CF2 disks, CF2-DD disks,
CPS8256 interface, *'Soft 160
Guide to LOGO'* by Boris Allen
(Chairman of British LOGO
User Group) and dust cover for
your PCW are all available.

Caxton Software Ltd
Lading House
10-14 Bedford Street
London
WC2E 9HE
Tel: 01 379 6502

Producers of Brainstorm, the
powerful organiser that should
have been used to write this
book! A good example of
software prices cut to
match Amstrad's.

CP/M Users Group (UK)
72 Mill Road
Hawley
Dartford
Kent
DA2 7RZ

Run by amateurs for amateurs.
It has maintained a library of
public domain software since
1981. Contact them for
membership details.

Database Software Ltd
Europa House
68 Chester Road
Hazel Grove
Stockport
SK7 5NY
Tel: 061 429 8008

Mini Office II. Amazing
low cost good value software.
Word processor, Database
Spreadsheet, Graphics
Communications and
Label Printer.

Database Publications Ltd
address as above
Tel: 061 456 8383

Organisers of the regular
'Amstrad Computer Shows'
in London and Manchester

Dictaphone Company Ltd
Regent's Square House
The Parade
Leamington Spa
CV32 4NL
Tel: 0926 38311
Ask for the Amstrad Hotline

Maintenance covering mainland
UK. Contact them for current
costs. Includes parts, labour
and on-site maintenance. They
can supply and install 2nd
drive but not CPS8256
interface or memory upgrade.

Digital Research (UK) Ltd
Unit 12
Fenton Way
Southfield
Basildon
Essex
SS15 6SL

Creators of CP/M, DR LOGO,
DR DRAW, DR GRAPH, etc.
Official CP/M Manual costs

Garwood (Wholesale) Ltd
45 Plovers Mead
Wyatts Green
Doddinghurst
Essex
CM15 0PS
Tel: 0245 460788

Suppliers of printer stands,
CP/M software, disks, ribbons,
computer labels, disk storage
boxes, dust covers and listing
paper.

Grey Matter
4 Prigg Meadow
Ashburton
Devon
TQ13 7DF
Tel: 0364 53499

They provide a disk copying
service at a very reasonable
cost. If you have already
bought software for another
computer they might be able to
convert it to suit the PCW.

Hunterforms
Lion House
Tidy Industrial Estate
Ditchling Common
Hassocks
West Sussex
BN6 8SL
Tel: 04446 47516

Business forms supplier.
Pre-printed continuous
stationery of all kinds
including micro-perforated
letters, invoices, cheques,
payslips and computer labels.
Also ribbons, disks and a
wide range of accessories.

NewStar Software Ltd
200 North Service Road
Brentwood
Essex
CM14 4SG
Tel: 0277 220573.

Pioneers of low cost software
for the PCW. Their catalogue
is combined with that of
Software Toolshop Ltd.
Includes software from
Saxon, Caxton, Sorcim,
Microsoft, Comshare, Camsoft,
Sage, Ashton-Tate, Iansyst,
Infocom, Abersoft, HiSoft,
Digital Research, Arcom,
Delta, Borland, MicroPro,
Prospero, Manx, Nevada, Aztec,
Zedcor, Locomotive Software,
BDS, Oasis Systems, LPA,
and Poor Person Software, etc.

Northern Computers Ltd
Churchfield Road
Frodsham
Cheshire
WA6 6RD
Tel: 0928 35700

Specialists in networking.
Also suppliers of a 20M byte
(equivalent to 114 disks)
hard disk storage system.

PCW Users Group
37 Clifford Bridge Road
Binley
Coventry
CV3 2DW
Tel: 0203 441417

Independent group run by
Robert Mobberley. Aims are
to exchange information by
means of a monthly newsletter
containing reviews and
letters. Lots of practical
hints and tips plus useful
addresses.

Quest International
Computers Ltd
School Lane
Chandler's Ford
Hampshire
SO5 3YY
Tel: 04215 66321

4 week free of charge support
on installation of their
products. It is a pity that
more companies don't state
their terms this way. Quest
even offer evaluation packs
at a reduced cost.

RAD Systems
Business Technology Centre
111 High Street
Wealdstone
Harrow
HA3 5DL
Tel: 01 863 2559
Repairs
Tel: 01 863 0189

Amstrad authorised dealer and
repair centre. 2nd drives
either 3-inch or 5¼-inch.
Interface for daisy wheel
printer. Memory upgrades;
they will supply a kit plus
fitting instructions if you
feel confident enough to
fit the chips yourself.

SageSoft plc
NEI House
Regent Centre
Gosforth
Newcastle upon Tyne
NE3 3DS
Tel: 091 284 7077

Suppliers of accounting and
communications software. You
can rent a PCW plus Sage's
popular accounting and
database packages for a very
low cost (minimum one year).

Software Toolshop Ltd
180 High Street North
Dunstable
Bedfordshire
LU6 1AT
Tel: 0582 699657

See NewStar Software Ltd

The Miniature Tool Company   Suppliers of printer extension
26 Queensbury Street Parade   cables and disks.
Edgeware
Middlesex
Tel: 01 951 1183

Xitan Ltd   Their own CP/M software, plus
Xitan House   more from Digital Research,
27 Salisbury Road   Microsoft, Ashton-Tate,
Totton   EcoSoft, MicroCal, Abtex,
Southampton   Sorcim, MicroPro and Avocet.
SO4 3HX
Tel: 0703 871211

Appendix C Keyboard Characters

Key	\<SHIFT\>	\<ALT\>	\<ALT\>\<SHIFT\>	\<EXTRA\>
a	A	α		ª
b	B	β		ß
c	C			©
d	D	δ	Δ	†
e	E	ε		
f	F	ø		ƒ
g	G	γ	Γ	
h	H	←		
i	I	⊗	⊙	
j	J	↔		
k	K	→		
l	L	λ		
m	M	μ		
n	N	↓		
o	O	ω	Ω	º
p	P	π	Π	¶
q	Q	θ		
r	R	ρ		®
s	S	σ	Σ	ß
t	T	τ		™
u	U	↑		↑
v	V			
w	W			
x	X	χ		
y	Y	ψ		¥
z	Z			

Key	<SHIFT>	<ALT>	<ALT> <SHIFT>	<EXTRA>
1	!	⅛		¡
2	"	¼		¨
3	£	⅜		℞
4	$	½		¢
5	%	⅝	‰	°
6	'	¾		´
7	&	⅞		^
8	*	å	Å	`
9	(	æ	Æ	↔
Ø	)	ø	Ø	O
−	—	±		~
=	+	≃	≡	≠
[	{			
]	}			
;	:	∴		↑
§	<	≤	⇐	«
#	>	≥	⇒	»
,	,	Ç	Ç	
.	.	°	•	|
/	?	÷	×	¿
½	@	∞		\

ACCENTS. Type the accent (´ , ` , ^ , ~ , or ¨) first and then the letter. The letter will then be printed below it, for example like this ñ.

FRACTIONS. Additional fractions can be produced by using the superscript control code for the numerator and subscript for the denominator. For example using these control codes (:+:SupeR)1(:−:SupeR)/(:+:SuB)3(:−:SuB) produces ¹/₃.

<ALT>+<ENTER> alternately sets/clears UPPER case characters (except Greek).

<ALT>+<RELAY> alternately sets/clears the numeric keypad.

INTERNATIONAL CHARACTER SETS. Under CP/M the PCW's keyboard can be set up to one of eight characters sets: American, French, German, English, Danish, Swedish, Italian or Spanish.

Glossary

A

Applications programs. Software that is used for a particular application. For example word processors, spreadsheets etc.

ASCII. (American Standard Code for Information Interchange). Computers cannot store keyboard characters so all characters are given a code number; ASCII is a system for coding keyboard characters.

Auto-repeat. This is what happens when you press a character key for more than about a second. See rollover.

B

BASIC (Beginner's All-Purpose Symbolic Instruction Code). A popular high level programming language developed in the mid-1960's to provide an easy to use and learn interactive language for computer users

Benchmark. A series of programs that are run on a computer to test its performance in terms of speed.

Broken paragraph. A paragraph that is split between two pages.

Bundled software. The software that is supplied 'free' with the machine when you buy it.

Byte. The amount of storage space required to hold one keyboard character.

C

Characters per second (cps). A measure of the speed at which a printer produces characters.

Computer literate. Not a well read computer but hopefully what you will become by reading this book!

Control codes. Same as Embedded commands.

Control key (CTRL). A key which is often provided on computers and used in conjunction with other keys. It is normally provided on CP/M micros; it is labelled <ALT> on the PCW's keyboard.

CP/M. (Control Program for Microcomputers). The operating system most commonly used in 8-bit business microcomputers.

Cursor. A symbol on the screen which usually shows where the next character you type will appear. The PCW's *character* cursor is a small rectangle which flashes. Its *group* cursor is used to indicate the group name. Its *file* cursor is used to represent the filename. Its *menu* cursor is used to indicate the option that will be selected if you press <ENTER>.

Cursor control keys. The set of four arrow keys (⟨←⟩, ⟨→⟩, ⟨↑⟩ and ⟨↓⟩) which move the cursor in four different directions when pressed.

D

Daisywheel printer. A type of printer that produces high quality print from character shapes moulded on to a circular print wheel which is shaped like a daisy with each character on a 'petal'. Daisywheel printers cannot be used to print graphics.

Data. The information that you give the computer to operate on, as it follows the instructions in a program.

Database. A store of information arranged for a computer to handle.

Data disk. A disk that is used to store LocoScript documents but not LocoScript itself.

Dedicated word processor. A computer that is designed to be used only as a word processor.

Decimal tabs. Special tabs that are used to line up columns of figures so that the decimal points are aligned directly underneath each other.

Delete. To rub out or erase. It could be a character displayed on the screen or a whole document.

Disk. A flat, circular piece of magnetically coated plastic on which data and/or programs can be stored and retrieved using a disk drive. Usually enclosed in a cardboard or plastic sleeve.

Disk drive. A peripheral used to load (retrieve or read) and save (store or write) programs and/or data from/on disks.

Disk Operating System (DOS). A disk based program (e.g. CP/M) which tells the computer how to use its resources (e.g. the disk drives) as opposed to a Disk Filing System (DFS) which is ROM based (e.g. the BBC Micro's DFS). A DOS has to be booted into RAM before the microcomputer can be used whereas a DFS is available as soon the micro is switched on.

Display. The characters and/or graphics the computer puts on the screen or monitor.

Dot matrix printer. A printer which forms character shapes as a pattern, or matrix, of tiny dots. They can print both characters and graphics. The other kind of printer that is commonly used in word processing is the daisy-wheel printer.

Double-density disk. A disk which can be used to store twice the amount of data on one side as a single-density disk.

Double-sided disk. A disk which can be used to store data on both sides.

E

Electronic mail. The exchange of document files between computers or word processors via telecommunications networks e.g. telephone, satellite.

Embedded commands. A method of giving a word processor formatting instructions by typing them into the body of the text. On the PCW embedded commands are usually enclosed in parentheses. The word processor follows formatting instructions as the text is printed out.

Escape key (ESC). A key which is provided on many computer keyboards and is used in CP/M; this key is labelled <EXIT> on the PCW's keyboard.

F

File. A document or section of your typing which you save, work on or print out separately from others. Equally it could be a collection of ASCII characters (without any control codes) or just a program.

File description. A unique name which you give a document or file so that it can be identified by the computer once it has been saved. It comprises two parts: the *filename* and the *filetype* which must be separated by a full stop (or period).

Filename. A general term used to describe the name given to a file. More correctly, the mandatory first part of the file description. Maximum 8 characters excluding < > = ! ¡ * ? & / , [ ] ( ) . : ; \ + -.

Filetype. The optional second part of the file description. Maximun 3 characters excluding < > = ! ¡ * ? & / , [ ] ( ) . : ; \ + -.

Footer. The margin at the bottom of a document. Sometimes called the Footer zone or a trailer. See Header.

Format. The layout or arrangement of text on the screen to be printed out. Also the process of preparing a brand new disk for use.

Friction feed. A method of feeding paper through a printer by means of a platen.

Function keys. Keys on the keyboard which are used for special purposes. On the PCW they are used to invoke pull-down menus.

G

Graphics. Graphs, diagrams and pictures displayed on the screen or monitor.

H

Hardcopy. A printout of a document or program on paper.

Hard disk. A magnetic disk which is normally sealed in its drive and has a large capacity (many megabytes). Sometimes called a winchester or winchester disk because the technology was first developed by IBM at their laboratories in Winchester, UK.

Hardware. A general expression for the computer itself and any peripherals that are connected to it.

Header. The margin at the top of a document. Sometimes called the Header zone. See Footer.

I

Inserting. The process of typing characters between characters that are already on the screen. See overwriting.

Interface. A common boundary between two hardware systems, devices or programs. Any hardware and/or software necessary to get a computer to work with other hardware (e.g. the CPS8256; see Chapter 5).

Inverse video. Same as reverse video.

J

Jargon. What this glossary is all about!

Justification. The lining up of a column of text on both left and right-hand sides.

K

Keyboard. The part of the computer on which you type.

Kilobyte. A unit of measure used to define the capacity of a computer's memory and of peripherals used to store programs and data. 1 Kilobyte=1024 bytes.

L

Language. A code of letters, words, numbers and symbols, which is understood by a computer, that you use to program (instruct) it.

Load. To transfer data or a program previously stored on disk into the computer's memory.

LocoScript. The word processing software that is supplied with the PCW and which provides its own operating system.

LOGO. An educational programming language that involves moving a 'turtle' around the screen; LOGO is supplied with the PCW.

M

Mail-merge. Merge a file which contains a standard letter, either with data typed in directly or with data from another file. The data could be names and addresses.

Margin. Distance between edge of the screen or paper and the left-hand side of the page body.

Memory. The part of the computer or word processor which stores programs and data.

Menu. A list of choices or options displayed on the screen.

Microprocessor. A semiconductor component which contains the Central Processing Unit (CPU) of a microcomputer or word processor.

Modem (modulator/demodulator). A device which is used to convert computer data into a form that can be transmitted using a telephone and to convert it back into a form that can be interpreted by a receiving computer.

Monitor. High resolution display screen especially designed for use with a computer or word processor, which does not have the tuning circuitry required for TV reception.

N

Network. A number of computers which are connected together and that are capable of passing data from one to another.

NLQ. (Near Letter Quality). A term that is applied to dot matrix printers which produce print quality almost as good as daisy wheel printers.

O

On-screen formatting. System for giving a WP formatting

instructions. Text appears on the screen in the shape in which it will be printed out. What you see is what you get (WYSIWYG)!

Operating system. The programs containing instructions which tell the computer how to work e.g. CP/M. It needs to be loaded into the memory before the computer can do anything.

Orphan. The last sentence (or part thereof) which is carried over to the next page leaving the rest of the paragraph on the previous page. See widow.

Overwriting. Typing characters over characters which are already on the screen in order to replace them. See inserting.

P

Pan. Movement of text on a screen either to the left or to the right. See scroll.

Peripheral. Any piece of hardware connected to a computer e.g. printer.

Pin feed. Same as tractor feed

Pitch. Number of characters printed per inch by a printer. In LocoScript the pitch can be varied between 5 and 17 characters per inch.

Platen. A hard rubber roller used in friction feed printers.

Program. A sequence of instructions, in a computer language, which can be followed by a computer as it carries out its task.

Proportional spacing. The ability of a printer to adjust the space between characters as it prints them according to their shape, to give a neater appearance.

Pull-down menu. A section of the screen which acts like a roller blind with a number of options written on it. These menus are usually invoked by pressing a function key and may be cleared from the screen by pressing <CAN>.

Q

QWERTY keyboard. Most common type of keyboard, named after the first six letters on the top row of letter keys.

R

RAM (Random Access Memory). Where a computer stores its programs and any data it is working on. The contents of RAM are lost (unless saved onto disk first) when you reset the computer or when the electricity supply is cut off.

Repeat. See auto-repeat.

Resolution. How well-defined fine detail can be displayed on a screen or monitor.

Reverse video. A highlighted area of the screen or monitor.

Rollover. LocoScript operates a two key rollover for keyboard input. It recognises a second key press even while the first key is still pressed.

ROM (Read Only Memory). Non-volatile memory which is provided in some computers and used to store programs permanently. ROM is not used in the PCW; all of its memory is RAM (except the bootstrap program which is stored in the 8041 printer controller chip).

S

Save. Store (save) data or programs on disk or in memory.

Sans-serif. Letters without little 'twiddly' bits on their ends

Scroll. Movement of a screen full of text either up, down, left or right.

Search and replace. Method of exchanging one word or phrase for another throughout the text.

Shared resource system. Word processing system which comprises a number of terminals sharing central storage and printing facilities

Shift key. Key which you press together with a letter key to obtain capital letters. With number keys the top symbols are obtained.

Soft keys. Keys which you can program or reconfigure. See User definable keys.

Software. Computer programs which comprise a sequence of instructions to make a computer perform its task.

Spelling checker. A program that will cheque and corect your speling for you!

Spreadsheet. A program that maps out a grid of 'cells' made by the intersections of columns and rows. You can move a cursor to any cell and insert letters or numbers. You can also type formulae to get the computer to do calculations on the contents of cells either in rows or columns. Commonly used in accounting and financial planning.

Stand-alone system. WP which has its own disk drive(s) and printer.

Stand-alone. A term used to describe a computer which is not connected to a network.

Start of Day Disk. Same as working copy disk.

Switched bank memory. A technique that allows an 8-bit microprocessor to address more that 64K of RAM; as used in the PCW.

T

Tab. A point set in from the main left-hand margin by a specified amount, where lines can be started on the screen. Used for columns, starting paragraphs, etc.

Terminal. VDU and keyboard which shares other equipment such as disk storage or printers.

Tractor feed. Method of feeding continuous stationery through a printer.

U

User definable keys. Keys that can be programmed by the user. See Soft keys.

V

VDU. Visual Display Unit. Usually comprises a monitor; with the PCW it also houses the disk drive(s).

Verify. To check the integrity of a disk and/or its data. This is normally done by running a special utility program.

W

Word processor (WP). Computer which uses a program that lets you type in, store, retrieve, edit, and print out text.

Word wrap. Same as wraparound.

Working copy disk. A disk which contains a copy of LocoScript and used to store files that you are currently working on.

Wraparound. Automatic movement of the cursor to the beginning of the next line down on the screen when the previous line is full of characters.

Widow. A paragraph that is split between two pages in such a way that its last sentence (or part thereof) is printed on the second page. See orphan.

X

X-Y Plotter. A peripheral that is used to plot charts, produce drawings etc. It comprises two bars which can be moved along the x and y axes respectively and supports a pen to produce the drawing. Sometimes called a graph plotter or flatbed plotter.

Y

Y (yes). When using the Verify/Format/Copy menu, pressing <Y> instructs the program to start the process.

Z

Zeroes. In computing a zero with a slash (∅) through it is frequently used to avoid confusion with the letter O.

Zone. A section of the screen or document. For example *Control* zone or *Header* zone.

Index